Sweet Pecan Pie

SWEET PECAN PIE

Grab Your Slice and Say Yes
to a Life Full of Joy, Purpose,
and Adventure

Drew Dusebout

Ballast Books, LLC
www.ballastbooks.com

Sweet Pecan Pie
Grab Your Slice and Say Yes to a Life Full of Joy, Purpose, and Adventure

Copyright © 2024 by Drew Dusebout

ISBN: 978-1-962202-86-2

Printed in the United States of America

Published by Ballast Books
www.ballastbooks.com

For more information, bulk orders, appearances, or speaking requests, please email info@ballastbooks.com or visit www.ballastbooks.com.

TABLE OF CONTENTS

Foreword

by Vicki Dusebout

An unexpected thing happened as my husband was getting ready to publish his book—I got cancer.

* * *

Most of us know someone who has cancer, died from cancer, or beat cancer. We can all imagine people meeting with an oncologist and the sterile, colorless cancer center where people from all ages and walks of life sit side by side, rarely speaking, as the "poison"-like infusion is put in their bodies to hopefully send the dreaded disease into oblivion and remission.

But knowing someone is quite different from being the "one."

* * *

Throughout Drew's writings, I have been his key supporter, encourager, and amateur content editor, a role I am most comfortable in. Not that we don't support each other in our various endeavors—it's just that I don't enjoy being the center of attention. Drew is a bigger personality, more outgoing and comfortable in front of audience, but for me, it's really something I try to avoid. As I tell my kids, "I'd rather do a hundred hours of dish duty before speaking and standing in front of a crowd." So, putting my thoughts in print really is a stretch for me.

At first, early in my diagnosis, I told Drew to just go publish the book. Why wait? I will be fine. We both know it's not as if he is a well-known author, influencer, or famous person spilling the dirt in a tell-all life story. That said (with an obviously partial view), reading *Sweet Pecan Pie* will make you laugh, cry, and think about leading a more adventurous, purposeful, and joyful life. I know he wants to launch this labor of love by sending books to family and friends and to be able to share it with others in a wholehearted and unpretentious way.

As we processed this season of our lives, he made a good point: it would be hard to imagine reaching out to our friends about his book when they are all checking in and asking about me. It sort of conflicts with a message of the book—to live a selfless life starting with your wife and your kids. And as much as I don't want to admit it, this whole cancer trial has moved me from being the person who brings the casseroles, drops off the care packages, and sends notes and prayers to those who are hurting—to the one who could use some help, the one whom people are praying for and trying eagerly to serve. This shift in roles has made me uncomfortable, but it's also been beautiful in many ways, as I've been shown love by people who are angels right here on earth, over and over again, and am forever changed for the better because of them.

Talking further after my surgery, while waiting to heal before chemo started, we considered the idea that perhaps this trial should be a part of the book. At first, I wasn't thrilled about it. I didn't want to be a spectacle. So many people have it worse, and who needs more stuff to worry about? But as we sat together in some of the quiet, low moments, I was reminded that it's how we live in the tough times that impacts people the most, and that by sharing I just might inspire someone who feels like things are hopeless. So, can my story encourage others who are struggling?

I sure hope the answer is yes because here I am.

* * *

There are many songs that include some form of "bags are packed," and since Drew likes to weave pop culture into his writings, I will follow suit and share that John Denver's "Leaving on a Jet Plane" comes to mind. We did in fact have our bags packed, or at least in the entryway, waiting to be loaded in the car for our fall excursion into the Rockies.

I had a little blood in places we don't like to talk about much and was thinking it was from too much fun and time on my e-bike, so I scheduled a doctor's appointment the next day to check on things, assuming I would get a pass and off we would go.

A quickly scheduled colonoscopy followed to make sure all was OK—it wasn't.

The next thing I knew, Drew and I were meeting with the doctor, who handed me a box of Kleenex after the procedure and said, "I am so sorry." Instead of being on the road the next morning, we found ourselves in the surgeon's office discussing CEA markers, scans, and surgery dates.

Since the beginning of this season, our vocabulary now includes a new set of words that before all this were rarely part of our conversations: CT, MRI, margins, lymph nodes, second opinion, side effects, chemo, days off, blood levels, stage 3, and other terms made their way into the discussions, as much as I tried to avoid them.

* * *

I am, for the most part, an optimistic person, someone who has a deep faith, so I have felt that things would all sort out, that this was no big deal, and still do—even in the midst of my treatments, which, while not pleasant, are tolerable and certainly easier (in my mind) than for so many others whom I know or have seen at the cancer center.

At the same time, the rate of people dying is still 100 percent, so if this is going to be my time, I'm thinking, *Well, I had a good run down here and trust that Heaven is as magnificent as advertised.* I think this "peace that surpasses all understanding," as Philippians 4:7 describes, is that peace that comes from believing God is good and that there is way more to experience beyond this life, in Heaven, forever.

And I can tell you for sure that the greatest joy, even during the tough stuff, still comes, as Drew shares, from being purposeful and selfless. By no means am I saying that this has been easy or something I would choose or that I don't want to fully recover and live without that awful *C* word for the rest of my years. I'm just saying that I am doing pretty well, and I hope that in some capacity, I can be used during this trial to comfort and bless others and stay true to one of my favorite sayings that sits in sticker form on my refrigerator:

"Givin' is livin'."

* * *

In a strange way, all of this has been easier on me than on those around me, those who have shared this journey with me, those I love and care for so very much. Reflecting on those impacted the most—my husband, my kids, the rest of my family, and my dear friends—is bittersweet. All of this has made us closer now more than ever. Our faith has grown and strengthened as we know we need to lean on each other, trust God, and stay hopeful. I have seen a softer side of Drew. Much to his embarrassment, he cries more while I cry less—can't dream that one up!

He's shifted some of his priorities from all his "big-picture," "move-the-needle" ideas and plans to simpler, less recognized efforts— namely, serving me. I've now got a 24/7 manager, protector, advocate, supporter, assistant, best friend, and guardian angel as he has come alongside to help me do this, even stopping to be still and "smell the roses," as I often encourage him to do. The ways he has blessed me go on and on, and I know he feels like this is among his life's most meaningful assignments.

Drew has often said that for him and most guys, there are two sets of people with whom they would trade difficult places within a heartbeat, without hesitation—"Our wives and our kids." Perhaps the list goes on longer than this, but for Drew and most men, the short list is a no-brainer.

Reflecting on the obvious reality that he could not switch places with me was devastating to him. I imagine he has even had moments thinking about how life would look without me, although he never shared this out loud. Thankfully, after a bit of a rocky start, the tests have been more encouraging, and the news has gotten better. While none of us are ever promised another day, my prognosis looks promising.

* * *

As you dive into *Sweet Pecan Pie*, my encouragement is that you do so thinking about how a life lived well could look:

- That you don't pull back from the hard parts of life (and we will all have them) but rather see the good in all things and think about doing more and loving others more.
- That you don't forget that while some of the important things are heard out loud and are visible to a broad audience, often the really good stuff is seen by a few—maybe no one besides yourself and God, who I'm quite sure sees all things.
- That you understand, as Drew will remind you often, that true joy is not a result of our circumstances or found by gathering more stuff, but by choosing to live a purposeful, adventurous life.

In the words of one of my favorite sayings, my hope and my prayer is that you choose to "go the distance" with all you've got!

Introduction

As I peered down over the cliff, my stomach dropped at the sight of the steep crevice in front of me. After taking a step back, I carefully walked over to the garage-sized boulders that sat firmly in the ground on both sides of me—giant and immovable like they had been there for millions of years. It was a surreal moment as I put my hands on them, looking up at their sheer size, and wondered out loud, "How on earth did I survive this?"

No one was listening, as I was alone, back a few months later to check out the scene of the accident. I expect few people wander down the hillside in that area: it's too steep to hike, and the roads tend to wind around without much rhyme or reason.

Unless you live in one of the remote neighborhoods adjacent to the canyons, there's not much to do there except drive around admiring the views or use it as a "shortcut" to avoid LA traffic.

Unfortunately, the combination of hairpin turns, spectacular vistas and lack of guardrails claims its fair share of victims as drivers tend to go too fast or lose concentration, miscalculate, and fly off the road. They either go up in flames or, in the case of me and my buddies, hit a parked car on the side of the road that breaks our fall and saves our lives, settling us safely a hundred yards or so down the mountain, before the cliff drops off and the real danger begins.

It's crazy, a miracle really, that we all walked away pretty much unscathed, and I couldn't shake how close I was—how close we all were—to having our lives cut short.

Like most teenagers, my attention span was measured in minutes, and my priorities were self-absorbed, so even after visiting the scene I did not spend much time thinking about why we got off easy when so many others don't. But I do think deep down I did realize more than most my age that life is short.

The dialogue between "live for today" versus "save for a rainy day" has been around for a long time, and the way we are wired and our life experiences both contribute to which side of the scale we end up on.

Life is short when I was young meant "play, play, play." It still does to some extent, but at some point, when I moved from kid to grown-up, to a husband and father, this idea of living a life full of adventure morphed into living a life full of adventure and purpose.

Over the years, I have learned that for me, the greatest joy does not come wrapped with a bow but rather from the way I seek and love others. Took me a while to get there (too long really, as I am stubborn). But now that I get it—wow, what a ride it is.

My hope is that the pages ahead inspire you to live your greatest life to the fullest.

Life is short—make it count.

Chapter 1

Sweet Pecan Pie

If God had intended us to follow recipes, He
wouldn't have given us grandmothers.
—Linda Henley

Way back when I was a young man in my early twenties, I was strolling through a casino in Las Vegas—not a fancy, high roller type of casino but the type that those of us on budget might visit. The blackjack table closest to the walkway by the elevators was packed with an eclectic combination of folks, all seeking the thrill of beating the house and then sharing their exploits and good fortune with their friends or anyone else who would lend an ear.

I am not sure, but I think the minimum bet was $5 a hand, so this really was not the place where the professionals hung out, which was quite evident by the way this group played—no wonder the casinos make so much money. As I watched in amusement for just a moment, an entourage of loud folks who'd had a few too many walked by, and in a bit of spontaneity, one of the guys muscled his way onto the one empty seat at the table, pulled out a wad of cash, and decided to play. He never did ask for chips; he just put a hundred-dollar bill (or a few of them) on the table and, in a loud voice, bantered with the dealer about getting the "right" cards.

Here, he was clearly the high roller, a position he seemed to relish, and in a distinct southern accent would yell, "Sweet pecan pie!" in a long, drawn out way—think "Sweeeeet pee-con piiiiie!" every time he won a hand, followed by high fives and cheers from his new groupies at the table as well as his friends who loved playing vicariously through him.

There were more than a few "sweet pecan pies" thrown around in the fifteen minutes or so he lasted, and the image of him, a bit tipsy and sweaty from all the excitement, using this obscure phrase to celebrate, was quite the show. It's a picture or video in my head, to be precise, that has stuck with me for many years, so much so that I am still known to this day for yelling my own version of "Sweet pecan pie"—thankfully, not at a blackjack table (I am not a big gambler, never have been) but rather when I am about to take a few turns through the powder, head down the mountain on a bike, or embark on some other type of adrenaline-filled activity.

Despite its strange and somewhat unhealthy origin, the phrase "sweet pecan pie" said out loud has become a signature saying when my family and I are about to do something fun, much to the embarrassment of my kids.

Unfortunately for the gentleman who helped serve as a catalyst for this now time-tested Dusebout family tradition, each of his "sweet pecan pie" moments were offset by several "busts" or dealer wins, and his day after all that excitement ended rather quickly, the same way it does for most people who visit Las Vegas to try their luck:

With a lot less money than when he got there.

* * *

Most of the family-friendly movie *Cheaper by the Dozen 2* takes place at a fictional lake in upstate Wisconsin and revolves around two large families and the childish competition between the two patriarchs, who end up alienating their wives and kids in the process of one-upping each other. It is a silly, feel-good movie that does make several valid points about family and parenting, namely that there are no perfect parents and that us parents need to let our kids pursue their dreams, not ours.

Early in the movie, knowing that some of his children were now young adults and time together was becoming more and more sparse, one of the dads, Tom Baker, played perfectly by Steve Martin, persuades all twelve of his kids (that's right—twelve kids) for one last trip to the lake as part of a Baker family tradition. Watching him beg, bribe, and guilt all of his kids to show up is both a reminder of how far many of us parents will go to keep our families together and a nod to the importance of creating and celebrating traditions.

These family traditions take on many shapes and sizes: a special vacation spot like the Bakers' lake house, a board game that is played over and over, a certain meal that is served or a movie that is watched during the holidays, or even some ridiculous saying that gets repeated enough that it becomes folklore and is passed down through generations.

* * *

Pecan pie's beginnings can certainly be debated the way most things can be. Some say it was founded in New Orleans by the French. Others say a recipe was first published in 1898 in a church charity cookbook in St. Louis. Zac Brown Band's hit song "Chicken Fried" alludes to pecan pie being part of Georgian culture.

But regardless of its founding, there is little question as to where it has its roots. Travel through rural Texas and it would be hard to find a diner or restaurant where they didn't serve the world's "best" pecan pie. Pecan pie is so much a part of the Lone Star State that in 2013 they named pecan pie the state's official pie and have now adopted the pecan tree as its official state tree as well.

As one might imagine, growing up in a small town in southern Texas, my wife's grandmother, Myrtle, learned to make her family's version of pecan pie at a young age and then brought the recipe with her when she and her husband went west to build a life in Los Angeles.

The beauty of this tradition, like most traditions, is in the excitement and expectation that comes with it. Each year, right around Halloween, everyone in the family would begin to ask when Myrtle's famous pecan pie was coming:

"Do we get it for both Thanksgiving and Christmas?"

"How many will she make?"

And then in time, as she got older, everyone began with the inevitable questions about how exactly she made it so darn good. In her case, one could watch and participate, but Myrtle was old-school and held on to her position that no two pecan pies were the same and that measuring the ingredients took the fun out of it: "Just put in a little of this, a splash of that, and it all works out." This casual style, lacking any formality at all, frustrated the literal folks in our family to no end. But when we really get down to it, Myrtle's way of making each pie original, changing it up and making it a little bit different each time, and encouraging others to do the same is actually a pretty good metaphor for life in general.

If we are honest with ourselves, we are all looking for the perfect slice of the pie, a life full of joy, purpose, and adventure. But how do we get there? Can we just do the same thing over and over again? Can we just follow someone else's formula or copy someone else's recipe?

Here's the thing. We are all different. We look different, think different, and have different gifts, attributes, and deficiencies. Shoot, we ourselves are different at different times in our lives. So, by all means, let us learn from others to better understand the ingredients that make life taste so good. But let us also get after it in our own way, in a way that is uniquely us, and let's make it an adventure full of movement, full of something new.

In pecan pie terms, let's all find our own recipe and go for it.

Chapter 2

Who Are You?

As I have said, the first thing is to be honest
with yourself. You can never have an impact on
society if you have not changed yourself.
—Nelson Mandela

The English rock band The Who released their eighth album *Who Are You* in the summer of 1978, featuring the song by the same name. Written by band member Pete Townshend, "Who Are You," with its hard-driving rock sound and easy-to-follow lyrics, has become a staple of their live concerts ever since its debut. With colorful language and a few smashed guitars sometimes added in, it is the epitome of the classic rock encore.

Like most hit songs that stand the test of time, the meaning of the song's lyrics has been discussed frequently over the years. Many believe the writer was reflecting on his own life and the life of the band that he cofounded, wondering who he was—who they were.

I think this exercise of reflection and self-introspection is something we all can use at times. It is also something that we might do our best to avoid if we're running too fast or in the wrong direction.

* * *

I sat cross-legged on the floor in the study of a nondescript tract home in the West Hills section of the San Fernando Valley, sorting the contents of the office into one of three piles: keep, Goodwill, or throw away.

I am convinced that the cure for a pack rat (or "hoarder" as the new reality shows call it) is moving. What started two hours earlier as a thoughtful process with me looking carefully at each item and deciding which pile it belonged to was now a hastier, less discriminate exercise with me mumbling to myself, "I don't really need or want this." The black Hefty trash bag was now getting its fair share of items.

Taking the middle drawer out of the desk—the long drawer where we typically throw our paper clips, pencils, rubber bands, etc. I turned it over to dump the contents into the trash pile. (Who really needs more paper clips or staples?) But then, I saw it—there was a small 5 × 7 piece of notebook paper that was taped to the bottom inside of the drawer. The top part of the paper was folded over so I couldn't see it, but the front part had a bunch of numbers written on it. When I took off the tape for a closer look, I guessed that the left column was a list of dates (6/30/92 and so forth) and the right column was full of random numbers (60.56, 300, 900, etc.).

Puzzled a bit, I unfolded the top part of the paper. My heart sank; I sat there for a moment, tears in my eyes, and then I started to sob. Not the loud screaming cry but the cry from deep within my soul, the kind of sobbing that makes no noise and had me gasping for breath. I do not think I have cried this hard before or since.

With this kind of raw emotion, time stands still. We really never know how long it lasts, but at some point, my wife wandered into the room asking me how things were going. She is the hard worker of the two of us and was on a mission to get the job finished. Seeing me on the floor inconsolable, she rushed to my side and asked me what was wrong. I handed her the note; she knew right away and just held me tight.

* * *

I grew up in a home that rarely or ever mentioned God, which was odd considering that my dad was given the God and Country Award as a Boy Scout, was a missionary for a time in Puerto Rico, and had been a youth minister all before I came along. My mom came from a family that didn't go to church and she didn't want to become a minister's wife, so into the business world my father went. By the way, I don't have any angst about the path my parents took, but in hindsight, I feel like perhaps my dad would have been happier and more fulfilled if he'd stuck with a life in ministry. Then again, if that had happened, my folks probably wouldn't have got married and I wouldn't be here. So, this isn't something I spend too much time thinking about, as all these what-ifs in life will drive us crazy if we let them. All in all, I've tried to keep my head down and press onward.

For most of my childhood, I lived with my parents and a younger sister in a white-collar neighborhood outside Seattle. We were not rich, but we were comfortable and certainly surrounded by affluence. My father worked for Safeco Insurance, and as a young executive, he worked and traveled a great deal while climbing the corporate ladder. He was a serious man, working most of the time, and we were not particularly close. My mom and dad didn't have a good marriage, and our family was dysfunctional in a fairly typical manner; we all pretty much did our own thing.

As happens in corporate America, politics got the better of my dad. His mentor and boss lost the battle to be the next president of the company, and it became clear that Safeco no longer provided my father with an opportunity to advance. I share this not because I am bitter; that is the way it goes sometimes, but this episode did shape my own career path.

This led our family to Southern California and a series of business endeavors for my dad that did not go particularly well. As my high school years were coming to a close and I was heading off to college, our family, always comfortable financially, was now in big trouble.

I think my sister got the worst of those years. I left for college and was away while she dealt with a series of moves and the constant threat of water and electricity bills or rent not getting paid.

If I am honest, I was a spoiled kid, thinking that my parents were supposed to provide me with a certain lifestyle, and I was angry when they could not. In college, my roommates and fraternity brothers at UCLA all seemed to have money, some quite a bit of it, and for the first time in my life, I had none. My savings from a cowboy hat business, student loans, and working for $10 an hour in student health helped pay for my education and gas money for my moped (and eventually my old, beat-up Honda Civic).

I found myself jealous and bitter that some of my friends went home to Newport Beach or to their family homes in Palm Springs over Thanksgiving while I stayed and worked. Life was not (is not) fair, but in hindsight, I can look back and understand that these experiences were exactly what I needed. We grow the most through adversity, and it was during my college years that even amid the fun (and I did have fun, too much fun), I began to learn about work ethic.

As my college years came to a close, I got a job working at Drexel Burnham, which at the time was a high-profile investment bank. Graduation led to work and a training class in New York City. Fifteen hundred dollars a month plus expenses and a hotel room adjacent to Central Park; I had arrived!

Of course, New York City is expensive. So, thirty days later, I returned to Los Angeles to start working with no money and my first slice of credit card debt.

Still not completely serious about work or life but enjoying some of the spoils as a young hotshot stockbroker, I worked, went to happy hour, played softball, and lived in a high-rise apartment in Beverly Hills.

My roommate and I could only afford a place with one bedroom, which we shared, but we had a doorman and the rock star Joe Walsh lived above us. On the outside, I looked like I was part of the "scene" but still drove an $800 car and owned only one suit and two pairs of dress socks.

Eventually, I decided that somehow, some way, I would get rich. Upon reflection, I was chasing what many young people chase: the American Dream—money, status, and the spoils and power that come with financial success. I was motivated by the understanding that I was on my own with no parents or family that could provide me with a safety net.

It was about this time that I met Vicki. Yup—she was the one, and I knew it right away. As early as our second date, we talked about life, family, kids . . . you name it.

Eventually, some success did come my way—not movie star, Silicon Valley, or hedge fund success, but success nonetheless, and with it came exotic company-sponsored trips, a couple of Mercedes, and a cool old Tudor home in the Los Feliz area of Los Angeles. Back in those days, I looked much younger than my twenty-seven years, and I remember a door-to-door salesman knocking on my door and asking me if my parents were home when I answered. Rather than say, "Why, no, they're out for the evening," my ego led me to tell him, "This is my house." (Note to self: pride leads to stupidity, and I ended up listening to his five-minute pitch on the value of his new, innovative, and life-changing suite of cleaning products.)

At the same time my career was thriving, my father was struggling. As an insolvent man now in his late fifties, he could only get jobs that paid by commission. You are either a salesman or you are not, and my father was not. Now in my fifties, I understand that the only way you can get a high-level job at this age other than owning your own business is if you do not need a job. Once again, I am not bitter about this or mad, just sad for my dad.

His struggles led to long conversations in which he asked me for advice and ultimately for a loan. I am embarrassed to admit this now, really ashamed, but I didn't respond to his request well. I was resentful. I was building my life, and parents are supposed to support and give to their kids, not take from them, right? He was "bumming my high" and slowing down my dreams.

Ultimately, I lent him the money, reluctantly and with a hard heart.

Vicki and I were in the wedding season of life and returned home one night from an engagement party for some friends at the posh LA Country Club to fifteen messages blinking on our answering machine. (Yes, this was before cell phones, and yes, I am that old.) Seeing that many messages, especially since we were only gone a few hours and with most of our friends at the party, I knew something was wrong.

The messages were desperate, hysterical calls from my mom. My dad had had a massive stroke and was in the hospital on life support. Following a somber, surreal thirty-minute drive across town to the hospital, we found my mom a basket case and my dad lying in bed with more tubes connecting him to machines than I could count.

My mom has never been able to handle adversity well, and this was as adverse of a situation as one could get, so I found myself, the cocky young business guy, in charge of making decisions about my father's life. I wasn't prepared for this (I am not sure anyone is ever prepared for this), but my grief and time consoling my mother was interrupted by the neurosurgeon in charge.

While I have no idea as to his level of skill or competency as a doctor, let's just say he was severely lacking in bedside manner. He hastily explained that my dad's stroke was a bad one, and while there was some chance that he could improve and have a decent quality of life, there were no guarantees. As he pushed us for a quick answer, we sat for a moment in shock. The circumstances were overwhelming, and the decision about whether to remove the tubes from my dad was something that I hope no one ever has to go through.

Ultimately, we decided that with even a small chance at quality of life, we would keep him alive and hope that he would recover from his stroke. The months that followed were some of the most stressful of my life. With my dad not having any insurance (he simply could not afford it and let it lapse), I found myself living through the bureaucracy of Medi-Cal and accumulated a mountain of files and notes on how to navigate the government healthcare system. I had files on different ways to rehabilitate from a stroke and entered into what became an intense tug of war between our social worker, who advised us to keep my father in the hospital, and the hospital, which wanted him out and into a nursing home. My days consisted of working twelve hours and then driving across town to see my dad and mom and deal with the never-ending forms and decisions. Vicki would wake me in the night, my T-shirt drenched in sweat from the stress.

After finally moving my dad into a nursing home and visiting him for a couple of months, Vicki and I came to the realization that my father was never going to get better, that he was never going to leave the nursing home, and that he was never moving back home.

So, I found myself sitting cross-legged on the floor in my dad's old study in his rented tract home in the West Hills section of the San Fernando Valley, cleaning out his belongings.

The numbers on the left side of that small notebook paper were, in fact, dates, and the numbers on the right side were dollar amounts. At the top of the page was one short phrase written by my father that wrecked me, that God used to soften me:

"Debts owed my son."

I think about the burden my father carried, owing a debt he could not possibly pay, and the lack of grace I showed him by not releasing him from that burden. I think about the condition of my heart back then and the fact most of my pursuits up until that moment in my life were all about me and what I got out of them.

In most cases, change is incremental, and this was no exception. It wasn't like this raw tug at my conscience meant "lightning struck" and I woke up the next morning a radically generous dude. But upon reflection, I think that it is this moment, full of shame, that served as a catalyst toward me living a more selfless, more purposeful life.

So, who am I now? Still a work in progress (I think we all are), but certainly not the same guy I was back when my father was struggling.

And that is my hope for all of us: that we take the time to check ourselves, to be honest and decide who we really are, not in some defeatist way, but challenging ourselves in the moments when we fall short and celebrating the victories when we take a leap forward.

My path has not been a straight line, more of a "two to three steps forward one step back" kind of journey. Yet along the way, it is in these moments when I mess up that I grow the most. I have learned that this is when God does His thing and offers us unconditional love and grace while at the same time prodding us along to do better, to be better.

Who are you?

Chapter 3

I Must Be in the Back Row

So the last will be first, and the first will be last.
—Matthew 20:16

In the 1980s, there was a series of commercials that did a good job of finding catchy ways to connect with their audience. Some of these commercials featured a journeyman professional baseball player named Bob Uecker who became quite well known as an announcer for the Milwaukee Brewers and a sometimes actor who had a way of delivering short, funny witticisms that were easy to remember.

One of his most famous catchphrases came during a commercial in which he is in his seat at a baseball game preparing to watch the game and talking about how ex-big leaguers like him get special treatment when the usher informs him that he's in the wrong seat. Uecker pompously remarks, "Oh, I must be in the front row." The punchline is that Uecker's seat was actually in the nosebleed section, the farthest seats away from the action as possible, where they pan to him sitting all by himself, yelling at the umpires. Since then, these back row seats have often been jokingly referred to as "Uecker seats" by sports fans everywhere.

* * *

While "I must be in the front row, oops, I am in the back row" has been a source of fun and mostly trivial conversation over the years, there's a more serious side to this topic. At times, it seems as if the world is divided into the "haves" and the "have nots." "A-listers" sit courtside, cut in line or skip lines altogether, and fly first class or alone with their sushi and pets while the rest of us are just happy to be there.

For most of my journey growing up, I sat in the "back row" and more recently have had both "back row" and "front row" experiences. If I am honest, I have to admit that the front row isn't all bad, although I also think most of the time, the people in the back row are more interesting.

I have also learned, as time has gone on and I have become at least a little bit wiser, that seeking the front row at all costs doesn't lead to happiness, and that too much "front row" living can be a dangerous thing.

There was an article in *Vanity Fair* written back in 2001 that provides a good illustration of the potential pitfalls of sitting in the "front row" for too long. The article highlights various socialites who frequented the island of Capri back in the day.

Capri, located in the Tyrrhenian Sea off the coast of southern Italy, is a small island (only about four square miles) and shoots out of the sea, with her limestone cliffs reaching heights of two thousand feet providing for a dramatic and unique setting. The island has always been home to the jet-setting crowd, a place where the yachts that dot the shoreline are measured by meters, not feet, and where the patrons are whisked to shore at night, taxied up the steep hills where they walk the cobblestone streets shopping for Gucci, Hermes, and Rolex before dining at fancy restaurants and then returning to their mansions on the water, ready to do the same thing the next day.

The article guides the reader through the history of Capri and shares about the lives of many of the famous people who made the island a summer home. While part of the article seduces us in a way that we wish we could be part of this privileged lifestyle, there is also an ominous tone to the stories about the dangers of living in decadence and without any real purpose.

There is a saying that has been around for years about the dangers of boredom, that "idle time is the devil's playground," and much of the story talks about the depravity that manifests itself in the lives of people who, on the surface, seem to have it all. The author paints this picture well and shares specific examples of the destruction that came with all the glamour in a way that is both funny and sad. The article ends with a quote from one of the characters from the story: "'Your brain go water, staying here too long,' she says. 'Too much paradise.'"

Too much "front row."

* * *

When I was twelve and living in the suburbs outside of Seattle, a friend and I shared a paper route to make a few extra bucks. The main paper in our area was the *Seattle Times*, and this was back in the days when just about everyone got that paper delivered Monday through Friday along with the more robust Sunday edition. We were in charge of delivering the local paper, which was only printed on Tuesdays and Thursdays and had a much smaller audience: about half the homes took the paper while the other half did not.

Our route took us through some wooded areas and included a series of new tract homes, a scattering of farms that were still holding on now that suburbia had invaded, and some larger homes on Lake Washington where the really rich folks lived. We divided the route based on the time needed to deliver all the papers, and my first foray into the business world was off and running.

Unfortunately, delivering to only half the homes presented a challenge—how do we remember who gets the paper and who does not? Our first few early mornings were a bit of a disaster, as we had to stop and check the list of our customers every couple of homes, which resulted in us both being late for school.

We needed a better plan. Being creative young entrepreneurs, we opted to get a couple of cans of bright pink spray paint. We needed bright colors since we were delivering papers when it was still nearly dark, and figured we'd just put a small dot on the driveways of the homes that were getting the paper. Genius! Well . . . not so much, as our early Saturday morning ride to get a system in place was defeated by the size of our pink "markers" and the fact that people noticed—including the elderly Mrs. Adams, who had insomnia, caught us in the act, and promptly reported us to our boss, the district supervisor. Turpentine helped get the paint off, and all this extra work probably helped our muscle memory become more familiar with who actually did subscribe to the paper, but the whole thing was painful and certainly not the efficient endeavor we had hoped for.

This was back in the days when getting paid was done via in-person collections, so once a month, we would knock on doors, ask for our $2.50 or thereabouts, hand out a receipt, and mark "paid" in our ledger. Looking back, this sure was a lot of work for not much money, but hey, you've got to start somewhere and pay your dues, I guess.

The collection process forced us to actually interact with a fair number of adults and provided me with a view into how older folks behaved that most people my age did not have. Some folks were super nice and generous, rounding up our monthly charge to $3 or even $5 in some cases. Generally, our tips were about the same as our pay (or even a bit more at Christmas time), and we eventually came to count on them as well as learn the value of being polite and providing exceptional service sans the pink dots.

Not everyone was friendly, and some were thrifty, but all in all it was a decent experience—except for this one man. I still remember him to this day. Let's call him Mr. Meanie because honestly that's what he was—mean. He lived in a big house at the top of what felt like the world's longest, steepest driveway. Mr. Meanie not only expected us to ride up the hill and put the paper on his porch but had a set of specific instructions on how the paper was folded and on which side of the door the paper needed to be. All this meant we had to get off our bikes and set the paper down in just the right way or be subject to his wrath and a formal complaint. I am not sure if OCD was a recognized thing back then, but Mr. Meanie clearly had some issues with order.

Collection time was also always a challenge with him. We would typically set out on our monthly collection task in the evenings around dinnertime or on Sunday afternoons when we would have the highest likelihood of finding people home. I swear he would see us coming and shut off all the lights or simply not answer the door. Getting what we were owed often required us riding up that driveway three to four times a month. Most of the time, he was without small bills, always pulling out a twenty and asking for $17.50 back, no tips ever forthcoming. And no way we could we bring him change later, either.

So, one Sunday afternoon, I'd had enough. He pushed me over the edge, and in my twelve-year-old brain, I wanted to get even—not in some sort of violent, go-to-jail kind of way, but in a way that would at least make me feel like I'd evened the score. Without spending too much time determining the optimum path of revenge, I settled on sneaking through the woods with my wrist rocket (think slingshot) and a smoke bomb. Fireworks were legal where I grew up, and you could buy a pack of six small smoke bombs in different colors that, once lit, would disperse colored smoke for thirty seconds or so and the Meanies would never be the wiser.

Harmless fun, or so I thought. Being a novice at this kind of thing, I probably put too much planning and misdirection into my journey over to the Meanies' house. I mean, it wasn't like I was navigating the streets of Beirut, avoiding spies in search of a hideout, or on my way to bank heist and checking for surveillance.

But there I was, looking over my shoulder on my trek over, a nervous wreck. I did all this planning to get there, but not much planning once I arrived at the large tree just outside the fence that surrounded their backyard. *What do I do now? What if they are not home? How long do I wait? What if they are home and in the house? How much time do I have? Can I launch more than one smoke bomb to make sure they know that they are "under attack"?*

Well, it turns out I arrived to the smell of barbeque, conversation, and laughter as the Meanies were hosting some sort of outdoor gathering. I couldn't see over the fence, so I tried to get the lay of the land by peeking through the slats between the wood planks, and while I couldn't be completely sure, it appeared that there were ten to fifteen people hanging out, mostly on the back patio. My first thought was, *Who would be friends with these people?* My second thought was, *Well, the stakes just got higher.* Smoke bombs are pretty harmless, and I certainly did not want to hurt anyone, but sending a smoke bomb into a backyard is one thing—sending one toward a crowd of six couples or so is a different matter. I could just see my actions leading to a handful of grown men chasing me down and either beating me up or holding me until the police arrived. *Maybe this isn't such a good idea.*

In hindsight, I should have just gone home and waited for another day. And if I decided to make my move then (which I did), I clearly would have been better just tossing the smoke ball over the fence and controlling the distance and keeping it away from the crowd. But hey, no guts, no glory, and there I was: ready, set, go, pulling back on the wrist rocket and launching the smoke bomb over the fence, not waiting around, adrenaline pumping, scampering back into the woods, and with no one following me, excited that I'd gotten away with a modest caper.

Turns out, as a matter of luck or fate, the smoke bomb went a bit further than anticipated, landed near the crowd, and hit a rock that was part of a round boundary that separated a big Douglas fir tree from other parts of the yard. It ricocheted over the lawn onto the patio and then rolled through the small opening in the sliding glass door, which just happened to be open, and landed on the Swedish hardwood floor in their dining room.

I probably would have never known all this happened and no one would have been the wiser except for a little girl from the neighborhood who saw the whole thing and, being a busybody and a bit of a pain (or morally grounded depending on your point of view), decided to tell on me. All that hard work to go unnoticed was to no avail.

Multiple phone calls ensued, and a few days later, I took the dreaded walk of shame up their driveway to deal with the consequences of my actions. Mr. Meanie opened the door, dressed formally in a coat and tie (didn't this guy ever just relax a little bit?), alongside his wife who I had never met before . . . and wish I never did. I quickly became aware that this was not one of those marriages where opposites attract; before I even had one foot in the front door, she launched into a tirade, which was a blend of her reminding me of all the beautiful things in her home and my despicable behavior.

Eventually we made our way to the scene of the crime, the dreaded dining room and the imported Swedish hardwood floor. While not being physically dragged into the room, I felt like I was being marched in there for my execution by force of personality, without any say in the matter. My smoke bomb actually sat in a bowl on the dining room table as if it were high-value evidence to a murder scene, the bright orange color now dulled with black soot from the smoke. There, in the corner of the room on the floor, next to some sort of hutch that held their fine China and expensive silverware, were a couple of small dots, not quite microscopic but pretty darn close.

I actually used the word *darn* when saying I was sorry for the umpteenth time and commenting that I was thankful that my actions did not cause too much damage. This really set Mrs. Meanie off again, as she lectured me that in no uncertain terms were they going to overlook these marks, that I was financially responsible to replace or restore the planks to pristine condition, and, furthermore, that my language and actions were surely going to send me to hell and that my kind had no place in her church.

I remember listening to her, thinking, *If this is what church people are like, no thanks.* Seriously, "darn"? It wasn't like I used the F word or anything. And sheesh, it was a smoke bomb, not a real bomb. Come on.

Mercifully, she stopped, probably because she was tired and out of breath. I scurried out, promising to pay for everything, which I did thanks to a series of lawn mowing jobs and a little help from my parents.

For the next twenty years or so, this was my impression of people who went to church. In Bob Uecker's words, not only did these people not want me in the front row, they didn't even want me in the back row or the parking lot for that matter. (And by the way, that was OK with me. Who wants to hang out with Mr. and Mrs. Meanie?)

* * *

Shortly after our first child was born, Vicki and I moved from Los Angeles to Santa Barbara. Soon after we arrived, some local families told us that we'd better hurry up and put our son, Spencer, on the waiting list for preschool. This seemed unnecessary, as he was only six months old, but not wanting to miss out, we listened and got him a couple of lists, including one for ELMO (short for El Montecito Early School), which, according to the folks we talked to, seemed to be a school that was always near or at the top. A few years later, there he was with a bunch of other three-year-olds, enjoying life and taking his first step into the world of formal education.

ELMO operated on the grounds of a church and was technically part of the church organization but with a fair amount of independence. Still suffering from PTSD over the whole Mr. and Mrs. Meanie encounter, I had a few flashbacks wondering if my son would get yelled at for coloring out of the lines or some other minor offense. But, as one might guess, that never happened. The teachers were just wonderful, which I am sure is the way things are at most preschools and certainly was the case here.

Prayer was certainly part of the ELMO culture. School started with a prayer, and assemblies, meetings, and events also included prayers. This was new to me, as most of my conversations with God over the years were negotiations with Him over something I wanted. Probably not as self-centered and manipulative as in the story below, but not completely on the up and up either.

* * *

There is a guy drowning in the ocean, with big waves crashing against the rocks and seemingly no way to get to shore. He cries out to God, praying and bargaining along the way, "God, if you save me, I will be a better person, a better husband, and stop stealing from my customers. I will never cheat again. Please just save me." All of a sudden, a giant wave picks him up and delivers him safely over the reef onto the small sliver of sandy beach between the rocks. Now safely onshore, the guy says, "Never mind, God. I got this one on my own."

* * *

The prayers at ELMO were different: trusting and soothing. One day, as I was picking up our son, I made a wrong turn and ended up in a classroom where several of the teachers were holding hands and praying for all the kids. I quietly observed them from the door for a quick minute, not wanting to interrupt but also not wanting to lean into something private. Hearing them mention our son's name, praying for his health, for him to be happy, for Vicki and me to be good parents, and for them to teach him well so he would grow up full of character and wisdom—this really got to me and painted quite a contrast to the way I prayed on the rare occasion when I talked with God.

* * *

Kids—especially when they're young—play a major role in who we as adults hang out with. With Spencer now in school, we got to know a whole new set of people whom we would get to see on a regular basis. Most of our activities centered around play dates with the children involved, but every now and then, we'd have some adult time with other couples of just the guys or the gals.

These were my kind of people; listening to Mick Jagger sing "Start Me Up" as we hopped on our bikes, kayaked in the surf, or even went free diving in the kelp beds off the shore.

Our activities usually included a dose of deep discussion about raising our kids the right way, and some of the guys prayed on occasion but not using fancy words or in an overbearing manner that made the rest of us uncomfortable.

As time went on, the topic of church came up. Most but not all of us dads seemed to regularly go on Sundays, or at least part of the time. I was in a place where I felt comfortable sharing about my encounter with the Meanies, an encounter that led me to run away from, not toward, the church for the last twenty years. Some of the guys actually laughed and high-fived me for having the ingenuity and moxie to actually fire up and send the smoke bomb into the backyard of my nemesis.

One dad, who was older, didn't have young kids, and wasn't a regular in our group, looked at me, shaking his head. *Uh oh, here it comes. Mr. Meanie is back in another body.* But instead, he said softly, "You know, Drew, there are plenty of angry, ugly people in the world, and the church has its fair share. Sounds like you found yourself a couple, which is a bummer."

He suggested that I look into the life of Jesus rather than the lives of people in the church. He told me how Jesus was most critical of the stuffed shirts of His day, the Pharisees, who claimed moral superiority as if, somehow, they were ordained to have all the answers, looking down on the rest of us who did not always get it right. Sure sounded like the way the Meanies treated me.

He shared from the Bible about how Jesus spent time with the nameless woman at the well who was of questionable reputation and an outcast in her own society. He talked about how Jesus drove the religious leaders crazy by dining with the vilified tax collectors and others who didn't always live "perfect" lives. Sure seems like Jesus was hanging out with the likes of me and my new friends.

* * *

Listening and reading a whole bunch, I came to believe that Jesus wants us to create a ruckus, not necessarily in the form of a rogue smoke ball, but in a way that is alive, fun, and not focused on adhering to a rule book, some formality, or a rigid behavior test. In the words of Bob Uecker, Jesus invites me—He invites all of us, the ordinary and the lame, to sit in the front row alongside Him.

But not in the way the world thinks. Sitting in the front row with Jesus doesn't mean that I will necessarily be rubbing shoulders in the owner's box at the Super Bowl or flying across the pond in my own G-4. But I think sitting in the front row with Jesus gives me something much more valuable: a sense of belonging, an understanding that I matter, that we all matter, regardless of what Mr. and Mrs. Meanie or anyone else may say. A-listers, are you listening?

"I must be in the front row."

Chapter 4

Game Time

Leave it all on the field.
—Vince Lombardi

I am a huge fan of playing games, anything from backyard hoops to ping-pong to backgammon. They are often the glue for families to stay connected. Right now, our family is into Apples to Apples, cribbage, and Catch Phrase, but when I was young, in the good old days, we played board games like Monopoly, Stratego, and The Game of Life.

Like Monopoly, the winner in The Game of Life is the player who ends up with the most money, the most assets—the *most*. Is real life that simple? Is it about getting more stuff? Is the popular slogan from the 1980s, "He who dies with the most toys wins," really the way to go?

I figure if fame and fortune are the answer, then why are so many famous folks on their third marriage, in rehab, or estranged from their kids?

As I think about it, in this game of life, the real game of life, each of us has the following:

- Time
- Talent
- Influence
- Treasure

And how we use each of them provides a glimpse into who we are and what we value.

Or, taking a slightly different approach, as my friend and mentor Bob taught me, we all have different aspects to our lives:

- Personal: physical, mental, and spiritual well-being
- Family: spouse, kids, grandparents, grandchildren, etc.
- Career/finances: what we get paid for
- Calling: what we are made for

There is an oft-repeated saying, and I am not sure who coined it first, but it goes something like this: "No one looks back on their life and wishes they spent more time in the office."

That is why this idea of where and how we spend our time, our talent, our influence, and our treasure is so important. That is why we must be honest with ourselves about how we are doing. That is why we must seek—no, actually demand—accountability from others, our spouse, our close friends, our mentors.

Getting this right, I believe, is the secret to leading a life of significance, a life of meaning.

* * *

In 1998, Molly and George Greene were operating an environmental engineering company in Charleston, South Carolina, when they heard about the devastation in Honduras caused by Hurricane Mitch.

After receiving a request for multiple water treatment systems in Honduras and being unable to find existing systems that would work,

George, Molly, and their team of engineers took action to build such a system, and thus, the idea for Water Mission was born.

When the Greenes arrived in Honduras, they were shocked by what they found. The river that flowed through a nearby village they visited was the color of chocolate milk, deep brown with toxins, bacteria, and hopelessness. The residents of the village referred to it as the "River of Death." No one survived once they drank from that river. As one of the newly built water systems became operational, the local villagers were still terrified to drink any water from the river, whether it was clear or not. So, Molly and George placed their own lips to the hose and drank the newly purified water. With that action, Molly and George bridged the final gap, and the villagers swarmed forward to drink the water.

In the aftermath of their Honduras trip, Molly and George discovered the sad truth about the global water crisis: that billions of people around the world are forced to drink dirty water each and every day. In response to this reality, the Greenes formally launched Water Mission in 2001 with the vision of all people having sustainable access to safe water, as well as an opportunity to experience God's love.

Today, Water Mission is a $20-million-plus nonprofit organization providing safe water, sanitation, and hygiene solutions to developing countries and disaster areas. To date, they have helped people in fifty-six countries and have over 350 staff members working around the world in permanent country programs. Having worked alongside them for a number of years, I know they are just getting started.

There is a saying: "When you see a need not being met, well guess what? It is probably up to you to meet that need." I'm glad George and Molly Greene got the memo. And while Molly went to Heaven a couple of years ago, her legacy lives on forever as someone who committed her life to doing the hard things, the important things.

* * *

As South African natives, Ryan and Gerda Audagnotti witnessed first-hand the devastation from the HIV crisis. They understand that many of the millions of orphans in that country and other sub-Saharan countries are orphaned as a result of the AIDS pandemic.

But Ryan and Gerda didn't run away from this tragedy. They didn't isolate themselves and their family from the reality or pretend it wasn't that bad or didn't exist. Instead, they ran toward it and, in 1998, started Acres of Love to rescue orphans and create families.

By creating "forever homes" with full-time house parents, Ryan and Gerda and the entire Acres team are able to not only provide for the physical needs of the kids they rescue but also their emotional and spiritual needs, the way it should be.

Not only did they run right into the crisis, they often ran right toward orphans with special needs, those society often tries to hide, welcoming children who suffer from abuse, HIV/AIDS, autism, Down syndrome, paralysis, hearing loss, and extreme malnutrition. None of this sounds easy—it actually seems overwhelming. But these special people do not look at the statistics and feel overwhelmed. They see each child as I believe God sees them: unique, beautiful, and perfectly created.

For years, Vicki and I supported this important work and had the honor to visit their kids, who have become our kids too. We have played together, gone out to dinner together, and visited an amusement park together, like one big family, at least for a few days.

Mother Teresa once said, "The hunger for love is much more difficult to remove than the hunger for bread." Hence the name: Acres of Love.

* * *

In Shelene Bryan's book *Love, Skip, Jump,* she starts off by sharing about the day her life changed. Shelene and her family had supported two children from Uganda, a girl named Omega and a boy named

Alonis, by donating $25 per month for each child to help with food, shelter, and the basics.

One night during a party at her house, one of the guests pointed at the pictures of "her kids" on the refrigerator and boldly said, "You fell for that?"

A few moments of uncomfortable conversation ensued in which the woman challenged Shelene that the whole thing might just be a scam, that there were no kids. It just was an effective way to raise money. Wanting to believe it was real, Shelene ultimately decided she needed to find out the scoop for herself, and a few months later, she left her comfortable life in Southern California and set out for Africa. Forgetting all the safety tips that she had read about and was committed to follow, she soon found herself walking a couple of miles through the jungle with people she had just met until they finally arrived at Omega's house, which really wasn't a house as we think of a house, but rather a mud-walled hut the size of a closet with a tattered sheet for a front door.

There she found Omega, bigger now but definitely the girl in the girl in the photo on Shelene's refrigerator back home. And there, right in front of her, stuck in the mud wall of this small room, was a Christmas card and picture of Shelene and her family. Overwhelmed by emotion and the realness of meeting a child she wasn't sure even existed, she hugged Omega and then said, "Omega, I will get you anything. What do you want, honey?"

Omega thought for a minute and answered, "I would like a bed," and two days later, Shelene, Omega, and Alonis, whom she'd now met as well, were in the bustling city of Kampala shopping. Not only did Omega end up with a bed, some sheets, a net to keep the mosquitos away, and some shoes, but Shelene—who was quick to catch on to the needs of others in the village—purchased every single bed in the store.

The store owner was overwhelmed with excitement and joy, letting Shelene know that his wife was pregnant, and that she surely must be an angel sent by God to help pay for the pregnancy.

As she shares in her book, experiencing the joy of others for what we in the US take for granted gave her chills. It was like God whispering in her ear, "You having fun yet?"

Seems that in God's economy, giving really is better than receiving. Thankfully, Shelene Bryan said yes and loved, skipped, jumped herself into a life of fun and purpose.

* * *

AP Economics sounds super exciting. "Micro" and "macro," graphs, balance sheets, supply side, Keynesian economics, and all sorts of theory. It is just part of the process: take the class, study, hope you get a good score on the AP exam, go to college, and (unless you are going to be an economist) forget everything you learned.

Enter Jamie DeVries, a teacher at San Marcos High School who challenged the status quo and decided it would be better to actually do economics and apply the principles learned than just sit in a classroom and, for the most part, get bored. Jamie founded Kids Helping Kids in 2002 and transformed AP Economics, a school, and a town.

Kids Helping Kids (or KHK for short), as the name suggests, empowers kids (the students) to invest in the lives of other kids needing socioeconomic and physical support, both locally and globally. This is done in a variety of ways but culminates with an annual benefit gala concert held at the world-class Granada Theatre in downtown Santa Barbara. The concerts are entirely student produced and have featured artists (some of whom are Grammy winners) such as Sara Bareilles, Switchfoot, and nationally acclaimed Andy Grammer.

They raise money to help children all around the world in variety of ways, including helping rescue girls in India from sex trafficking, providing clean water to kids in Honduras, and building a school in Rwanda. Locally, KHK helps families in crisis, including ones who have sick kids or have lost a child. They subsidize SAT and AP testing fees for students who are unable to afford the cost of the exams. And they do all this while learning to run an actual business and having fun in a high school economics class.

Maybe Jamie DeVries is on to something.

* * *

Brad Corrigan may be the biggest rock star you have never heard of. He and the rest of the indie band Dispatch have sold out some of the most storied venues across the United States, including Madison Square Garden, Red Rocks, Red Bull Arena, the Boston Garden, and Radio City.

But to know Brad and his story is to know that he is so much more than just a talented musician.

Ileana grew up in the La Chureca trash dump community in Managua, Nicaragua. As a child, she was prostituted to make money for her family. Brad met her on a mission trip in 2006, and his life changed forever. "That little girl became like family to me and wrecked me so beautifully . . . and I'll never forget the courage and strength in her smile."

Tragically, she contracted HIV and passed away in 2011, but Ileana's legacy lives on in the form of Love Light + Melody, a nonprofit organization founded and led by Brad that serves at-risk kids in that very same trash dump resettlement community where he first met Ileana.

When Brad says, "It's now my honor to speak and sing to her life so that other kids like her can be protected and live," he is certainly walking the walk, devoting much of his life to keeping her memory alive while changing the community where she lived—one child at a time.

Time, talent, influence, and resources are all we have. How do we use them? I think Brad Corrigan gives us a hint and set the bar high.

* * *

The best way I can describe Dennis Wadley is that he is a renaissance man of sorts. Pastor, entrepreneur, missionary. Whenever I hear from

Dennis, I am never quite sure what country or continent he's calling me from this time.

He and his wife Susan first learned about the HIV/AIDS pandemic through *TIME* magazine and subsequently made two visits to South Africa to learn firsthand about the effects of the disease. After falling in love with the people and the country, in 2003, the Wadleys assembled a team, received training, packed their bags, and, along with their three kids, moved clear across the world to Cape Town.

There, they partnered with a local church in Philippi, a devastated township of one hundred thousand people in the center of the Cape Flats, and founded a nonprofit called Bridges of Hope to train local leaders in the principles of grassroots, holistic community development. They set out to help these leaders and their communities experience God in a whole new way and be lifted out of the vicious cycle of poverty and disease.

As they worked with the ever-growing number of orphans and vulnerable children, the vision for Bridges Academy boarding school was born. In 2007, Bridges of Hope purchased a beautiful twelve-and-a-half-acre farm in Franschhoek, a peaceful community about forty-five minutes outside of Philippi, to use as a retreat center and school, a place where they could further their work.

Sometimes, the life of a full-time missionary gets romanticized. Like they're having tea and cookies in some fairy-tale setting. But the reality is much different. There is nothing overly romantic, or easy for that matter, about picking up and moving clear across the world, dealing with a new culture and never-ending crises, and doing so with three kids in tow.

My family and I paid a visit to Bridges Academy a few years back on our travels through Africa, so we were able to see much of what Dennis, Susan, and their team were able to do. We got to see the oasis they built in the middle of such sadness. We got to meet some of the kids they were helping. We got to travel into neighborhoods that they helped transform. We got to see the fruit of them risking everything to help change the world.

* * *

You probably noticed that none of the above stories were about someone building the hottest new tech company, having the most expensive home, or taking the most exotic vacations. It is not that any of those things are bad; I just think life is more interesting, more fulfilling when we run the race with God in mind, when we run the race for others than it is when we are comfortable and well fed.

Author and preacher Frederick Buechner wrote that "the place God calls you to is the place where your deep gladness and the world's deep hunger meet." This is probably my all-time favorite quote because it makes me think about what really breaks my heart, what really pushes me to take a risk, to sacrifice something big, because deep in my soul, I just can't let it go. It calls me to my sweet spot where the world's deep hunger and my deep gladness collide. It's the place where all the people in the stories above reside.

Here is the big news: Get in the game the same way as George, Molly, Ryan, Gerda, Shelene, Jamie, Brad, Dennis, and Susan, and you'll probably get dirty. You'll probably get bruised along the way and you probably will be uncomfortable. But as Warren Wiersbe, an American pastor and Bible teacher, once said, "If you want to be memorable, sometimes you have to be miserable."

Game time—are you in?

Chapter 5

Dream On

If you can dream it, you can do it.
—Walt Disney

This classic rock ballad "Dream On" from the iconic band Aerosmith first made its way to the charts in the summer of 1973 and still is played all over the world, not just in concert but as a backdrop at sporting events, motivational speeches, and presentations. I think the timeless nature of the song is because we can all relate to it in one way or another. As the band's lead vocalist, Steven Tyler, said, "The song is about the hunger to be somebody: Dream until your dreams come true. To strive to always be more doesn't mean that you are not OK with who you are. It means that you are open to learn better and eventually become better."

* * *

It is hard to forget exactly where we were on September 11, 2001. For many on the West Coast, people were still sleeping at 5:46 a.m. local time when the first plane slammed into the North Tower of the World Trade Center in lower Manhattan. This was back in the days when I was in the office early, and I still remember sitting at my desk alongside my business partners as the news began to pour out.

At first, no one was sure if it was a tragic accident, but as time went on, it became clear that we were under attack. Another plane crashed into the second tower of the World Trade Center in New York City, then another into the Pentagon in Virginia, and finally one in the countryside near Shanksville, Pennsylvania. This fourth plane was headed to Washington, DC, but thanks to the heroics of passengers on board, it was diverted to a rural area, no doubt saving countless lives.

Shock, dismay, and phone calls to loved ones to share the news and hear their voices followed. Calls to friends and coworkers in New York to make sure they were OK were often met with no answer or "all circuits are busy." Sitting in disbelief, unable to take our eyes off the news, most of our nation mourned and prayed together, waiting to hear word about those who were in the vicinity of the carnage.

As always, the first responders ran into harm's way, risking and in some cases losing their lives to help those still alive and trapped in the rubble. "Regular folks" within the vicinity of the attacks became heroes as well, leaving the comfort of their homes to try and help and serve in the aftermath.

9/11 was tragic beyond anything I'd ever seen, for sure. But it was also a time in which most of us forgot about our petty differences and annoyances and joined together, rooting for one another and living truly as the *United* States of America. It was a time in which we could all dream on, all dream big, and do so selflessly in unity.

* * *

There has been much discussion over the years about how to build a successful movement. Is it just the luck of the draw, or is there a science or art to building something that others long to be part of? Sure, you've got to pick a cause that inspires others to join, but I think there is more to it than that.

In Derek Sivers's clever TED Talk titled "How to Start a Movement," he points out that one of the main themes of successful movements or growing organizations is not caring about who gets the credit. It's all about getting to where we are supposed to go, not who makes the headlines. The talk involves an impromptu dance outdoors on a grassy hillside and makes me laugh out loud as well as learn this valuable lesson. If you want more details, you will have to go to watch it on YouTube. It is worth a visit.

And while the movement in Santa Barbara that started in response to 9/11 may not be as clever or whimsical as the one from the Derek Sivers video, I believe the idea of inviting everyone in as equals is one of the reasons it worked.

* * *

With the exception of Hawaii and Alaska, Santa Barbara is about as far away from New York City as any place in the country. For those of us three thousand miles from the madness, it became a struggle, not in the acute sense like so many who lost loved ones or were in the middle of it all, but in a different way—like, *How do we do something, anything to help? How do we take our prayers and our tears and turn them into action?*

Santa Barbara is a small town. It feels like everyone is only one step removed from knowing everybody else, and with this in mind, a small group of women decided to dream on and start a movement by reaching out to Pat McElroy, one of the chiefs at the local fire department.

Many of us around town know Pat, and we came to find out that his battalion had a sister battalion in New York City. This sister station, like so many stations in the Big Apple, had lost some of their squad in the aftermath of the Twin Towers collapsing.

There is a unique bond among firemen and firewomen and all first responders. I think there has to be in order to be effective when dealing with all the hardship they face on a regular basis; and as such, there was much emotion and grief in dealing with the loss of fellow family members.

So, our movement, this little movement that started with my wife, Vicki, and a few friends (Marisa, Joanie, and Marie), grabbed Pat and off it went. We secured the Earl Warren Showgrounds, Santa Barbara's only fairground that hosts the town's rodeos, carnivals, circuses, swap meets, and so forth, and set up a drive-through line where people could make donations to the firemen, who would then, in turn, send them to their peers in New York to help the families who lost loved ones.

The big marquee, which stands tall and is easily seen from the 101 freeway that passes through Santa Barbara, along with all the various forms of media highlighting the drive-through, made this a pretty big deal—the movement had grown from a few to a lot. People from all walks of life drove through and put checks, dollars, and coins into the boots of the firemen, which created some really cool imagery. Some people drove through just dropping off a donation, while others got out of their cars to shake a hand or give or get a hug.

Both the socioeconomic status and demographics of those contributing were wide ranging. From little kids selling lemonade to help, to the elderly coming in a van from an assisted-living facility, to the rich gal in her Rolls, to the restaurant worker driving his beat-up old motorcycle, it was one movement with one purpose, unified in heart and spirit.

One of the most meaningful moments for me happened when a guy in a pickup truck with a bunch of landscaping tools tied to the back stopped and endorsed his entire paycheck and handed it to a fireman, then opened his door, got out of his truck, and fell to his knees sobbing. The fireman got on his knees as well and held him, with tears streaming down both their faces. Truth is: tears were on all our faces.

In total, we raised over $86,000, which we sent (along with our three-foot-by-fifteen-foot banner signed by just about everyone who participated) with Pat back to New York to give to his friends and colleagues.

A few months later, he stopped by our house and gave my wife a beautiful book about 9/11 titled *Brotherhood*, signed by many of the firemen and firewomen in New York who were now our brothers and sisters. In addition to the signatures and kind words that were deeply personal in nature, the book is filled with photos and tributes, which really capture the devastation, the heroic actions of those who lost their lives, and the grief that followed.

Every part of the book is emotional; the pictures tell the story in vivid detail. We still keep a tab on a page 156, a tab we put in place twenty years ago when we first read the captions that accompany the visuals throughout the book, a page that reads as follows:

> "It's the custom of many fire departments at the funerals of fallen firefighters to have them played their rest by bagpipers. Sunday after the horror, beside a Hudson Ruby-Red in the setting sun, as near to the ruins as he could get, a lone piper was playing. He had no connection to the New York Fire Department; he wasn't even from New York. He was a guy from Boston, a plumber by trade, who happened to be a bagpiper and had been moved to tears by the heroism and self-sacrifice of our firefighters. So he'd come to pay his respects. At the time the exact number of fallen wasn't yet known, but it was put at about 300. The piper was playing a minute or so for each man, trying to keep each tribute a little different; plangent riffs on old Scottish and Irish ballads, songs of the lost love and the death of heroes and the longing for home. He's been playing for six and half hours. But each lament was sweeter and more haunting than the last."

* * *

Our family has been back to Ground Zero a couple of times and visited the 9/11 museum a few years ago. Like most memorials, looking through the events and reading the names of those who passed away is full of emotion. Let's face it, the world has plenty of tough, sad, unfair stuff in it, and 9/11 is near the top of the list.

Yet, it's during the really hard moments when people also rally. And 9/11, as tragic as it was, did serve as a catalyst, inspiring people to work together. It led to a spirit of cooperation that rarely happens when things are the norm, and it provided an environment where movements of diverse people, with little in common, could grow and flourish.

When I reflect on the journey our small town took, the biggest impact wasn't the money raised. Sure, $86,000 is a fair amount of cash, but in the grand scheme of things, in the midst of all the destruction and loss of life, I imagine we helped just a little bit.

The real beauty of our movement, our drive-thru, was the connection of people united in something big, something in which no one cared who was in charge. It wasn't about us, it was about those whom we never met, those who sacrificed more than we could ever imagine.

Let us all dream on, and not just on the big things. Let us think of others first. Let us join together. The world will be a better place because of it.

Chapter 6

Will You Be My Mommy?

Orphans are easier to ignore before you know their names.
They are easier to ignore before you see their faces. It is
easier to pretend they're not real before you hold them
in your arms. But once you do, everything changes.
—David Platt

The following story starts off as one of those "I know someone, who knew someone, who introduced me to someone, and guess what happened" kind of stories. The movies would call this a coincidence—or serendipity. I call it being along for the ride in a life full of adventure.

It goes like this: John introduced me to John and Kim. John and Kim introduced me to Bob. Bob introduced me to Jim. Jim introduced me to Joey and Mary and hundreds of orphans clear across the world.

Operation Christmas Child (OCC) and the delivery of shoeboxes to impoverished children all around the world is my wife's all-time favorite thing. Every year, she and hundreds of thousands of other families take the kids shopping for items to put in "our" shoeboxes so Samaritan's Purse (who oversees OCC) can collect and deliver them.

What had started years ago with our kids lobbying for their own stuff amid the shopping ("One toy for my shoebox kid and one for me!") had now actually become a selfless excursion, with them pleading for "just one more thing for my shoebox kid, please!" Allowances and babysitting money were even used to help make sure our shoeboxes were packed to the brim and loaded with good stuff.

Meeting Jim Loscheider for just a very short time led to a discussion about shoebox delivery. I offered some unsolicited advice about the benefits of making the shoebox experience more personal by connecting the shoebox giver to the shoebox receiver. Like many of my big-picture ideas, it was a decent thought but a logistical nightmare; although OCC does now allow us to track our shoeboxes to the general delivery location, so in this case, I was not completely lost or out of bounds.

Turns out Jim was kind of a big shot at Samaritan's Purse, and after exchanging contact information on Friday, I arrived home on Monday to an email from Jim suggesting that if I wanted to make OCC more personal, then why not have my wife and I join him and an OCC team to deliver shoeboxes in Ukraine that upcoming February. I really did not expect this and was super excited, as this was the absolute number one wish on my wife's bucket list.

But I also wanted to be polite, as I knew that shoebox delivery was the most coveted volunteer role at OCC. As much as we were dependable shoebox packers, there were plenty of people who donated more time and resources than we did who would also love to go on the trip, so I replied to Jim's email suggesting he really be sure before making such a generous offer, while at the same secretly hoping he would still invite us. He responded quickly: "I'm sure, come." And three and a half months after meeting Jim, Vicki and I were in Ukraine.

* * *

After Jim's invite, I got the kids together, swearing them to secrecy, and got a big cardboard box. Together, we stuffed the box with paper and put a shoebox in the bottom of it with a little note from me inside. We wrapped the box and, after dinner, told Vicki we had a present for her.

I am a lousy receiver of gifts and known in our family as the king of returns—not exactly a title to be proud of. Giving gifts is not my strong suit either. I am too pragmatic and tend to look at giving gifts from a cost/benefit analysis standpoint. Clearly, I have a heart issue. Vicki, on the other hand, is great at both giving and getting gifts. She is generous and even has a sticker on our refrigerator that says, "Givin' is livin'." She loves all the gifts she receives, or at least pretends she does with great authenticity. She isn't crazy about jewelry (which is good for me), but her passion and past career is interior design, so she likes nice stuff for our house (not so good for me).

We had a joke when we were in the furnishing our house phase of life. She would come home with some great stuff at a great price and say, "See what I got? Right place at the right time," and I would say, "Wrong place at the wrong time, and we're going broke saving money."

So, this present that appeared to be randomly given to Vicki in early November was a little out of the norm, and a big box full of paper was even more unusual. It wasn't until she read the note that she got it. Vicki cries at everything, even over a cat food commercial, so her tears did not necessarily mean that I knocked it out of the park, but when she kept saying, "We are really going to deliver shoeboxes, I can't believe it," I knew I got it right.

* * *

Ukraine in February is a little different weather-wise than winter in Santa Barbara, and we arrived in Kiev to a greeting from the Samaritan's Purse team that included some heavy OCC-issued fleece pullovers and jackets that were our uniform for the trip.

Vicki and I were part of the red team, and every morning our team would gather with our fearless leader, Joey, and head off to schools, hospitals, or orphanages to deliver shoeboxes and bond with the kids we were meeting. Other teams would do the same thing, and we would all reconvene back at the hotel each evening for a time of prayer and sharing.

Typically, we would make two or three stops a day, and every place we visited was unique and special in its own way. Each shoebox was packed for either a boy or girl and with a specific age group in mind.

The rule at Samaritan's Purse is that leaders can add to a shoebox if it is "hurting," but nothing can ever be taken out of a shoebox. The thought behind this rule is trusting that the right shoebox will end up with the right recipient. I heard about the time when a shoebox was packed with six pairs of tall white athletic socks and that was it. Common sense says, "Oh man, who is the poor kid who gets this box?" But as the story goes, the box was sent to a young boy who had scars on both his legs and had to walk through the snow to school each day. The socks both covered his scars and kept him warm.

Then there was the time the shoebox packer sent a necklace with the name Anna on it, and sure enough, the little girl who opened the shoebox was named Anna. That year, 8.8 million shoeboxes were delivered, and the box with the "Anna" necklace got to a girl named Anna. Gotta admit, it sure was fun to be part of these ridiculous, "are you kidding me?" moments.

It is hard to describe on paper the excitement our visits brought, but I still remember the kids giggling and peeking through the window and doors in anticipation of our arrival. But it was also impossible to miss the undercurrent of sadness and despair that the kids felt, that the house moms felt. On each of our stops, we would bring with us a pair of local comedians who spoke the language and would put on these skits for the kids, which were actually well done and over-the-top hilarious. And in the midst of the silliness, they made an important point—that God loves them and that each and every one of them is valued, important, and destined for a life of meaning. We were doing our best to give them something bigger than their circumstances to hold on to, to dream about, once all the excitement of this day was over.

It was during this trip that I learned that the shoeboxes OCC has the most trouble filling are the ones for the older boys ages ten to fourteen. Shoebox packers get to choose the age group and sex for their shoebox, and for most of us, it is just more fun to pack boxes for cute little girls or boys than for teenagers. Knowing this, I and some of the other guys on our team made a point of spending time with these older boys who were more sullen than their younger counterparts. Part of their attitude was just a normal teenage thing, but part of it was because they seemed to have settled in on the challenges that lay before them after their time in the orphanage. Adulthood as an orphan in Ukraine is a whole other challenge.

Having a son myself, I know that most guys love sports and balls of any kind, and they're all that is needed to provide hours of entertainment. So, we found the opened shoeboxes with balls, brought some of our own, and spent a fair amount of time tossing Nerf footballs, wiffle balls, and small plastic soccer balls over and through the crowds, adding to the chaos of the kids excitedly opening their shoeboxes all at once and even drawing the ire of the headmasters and house moms. As Vicki often says, "Drew is my fourth child," but hey, no one ever changed the world by following all the rules, and the laughter and high fives from kids we had just met were well worth it. It was like they got to forget about the reality of their lives for a while. They got to live like regular kids for at least a couple of hours.

On our last day, we visited an orphanage that just broke our hearts. Each bedroom had twelve to sixteen twin beds lined up side by side, and each bathroom had twice as many small cubbies, where each kid would have a cup and a toothbrush and their name taped on the bottom shelf so they would not get their stuff mixed up.

As we toured the home and chatted with the wonderful house mom via a translator, one little girl followed us everywhere, at first holding onto the skirt of the house mom, then eventually grabbing hold of Vicki's coat and ultimately her hand. She kept looking at Vicki and saying the same sentence over and over again. When my wife finally asked our translator what the little girl was saying, the translator got this resigned look on her face, hesitated, then told us that the little girl was asking Vicki, "Will you be my mommy?"

Each night after dinner and sharing time, Vicki and I would reflect on the day, how fortunate we were to be part of this shoebox delivery, and how determined we were to do more to help the widows and the orphans. This night, however, we just lay in bed and cried, overwhelmed by emotion.

All the OCC teams were given a color, and I'm sure everybody thought their team was the best; I know I did. There was even a friendly rivalry among the teams during share time. Each night, my wife would nudge me to stand up and say something in support of our team and our leader, Joey. One night, after I and several other folks shared a highlight from our day, a guy in front of me stood up and poured out his heart. He was a big man with lots of hair (these days, that makes me jealous) and a beard. By no means was he the most articulate speaker, and he certainly didn't understand brevity, but with tears streaming down his face, he shared how God saved him from a life of drugs and despair. His speech was rambling, raw, and unscripted. But by the time he was done, we were all welling up, and he ended with us all on our feet giving him a standing ovation. And I'd thought my talk was moving. Sheesh, I was just the warm-up act.

Heading back to our hotel room later that evening, we were joined on the elevator at the last minute by a slight woman with a warm smile. I had seen her in the back of the room throughout the week; she was memorable because of her consistent and rather vocal praising of God.

The sweet lady introduced herself as Mary, and I asked if this was her first shoebox delivery. She looked at me with a twinkle in her eyes and said, "Oh no, dear, I have been on more of these deliveries than I can count." We reached her floor and before she got off, she asked if she could pray for us. So with me holding the button to keep the doors open and the loud buzzer encouraging me to close the doors and get moving, she prayed and she prayed and she prayed. I was praying too; I was praying that the elevator would hold firm, not having much faith in the quality of Ukrainian elevators and certainly less faith than Mary, who felt quite at home praying wherever she was.

Not quite knowing what to think of Mary, the next morning, I found Jim at breakfast and asked him about her story. He was surprised that I didn't know who she was and proceeded to explain that Mary was one of the people who helped start OCC: first by traveling through rural Virginia collecting shoeboxes and showing up at Samaritan's Purse one Saturday with a U-Haul full of them, then by traveling to Bosnia during the war to deliver them, and ultimately becoming known as the "shoebox lady" and meeting with then president Clinton at his request.

Come on: first the little girl who wanted Vicki to be her mommy, then the bearded guy with the amazing testimony, and now Mary? I am not the most observant guy in the world, but I think God was trying to get my attention.

All of this is a great reminder of what happens when we say "yes" to a new slice of the pie—"yes" to a life of adventure. John introduced me to Kim and John, Kim and John introduced me to Bob, and Bob introduced me to Jim. Jim invited Vicki and me to Ukraine, and you now know the rest. The craziest thing? All this happened in a matter of months. Just imagine what could happen if we said "yes" all the time.

A footnote about Ukraine:

Seeing from afar all the destruction and loss of life in Ukraine as result of the Russian invasion, in places that we visited and affecting people we likely met during our time there, brings me to tears. It's a stark reminder of the evil that exists in the world today. Hearing about people who shifted gears, changed what they were doing in their daily lives to help others clear across the world, is a charge for us all to take action and run boldly into the injustices that break our hearts.

Chapter 7

Live from Bondeni, Kenya

And for me, I've realized that I used to be afraid of failing at the things that really mattered to me, but now I'm more afraid of succeeding at things that don't matter.
—Bob Goff

Once a quarter for three years, Bob Shank made the drive early in the morning to Santa Barbara from Orange County to do what he has done for thousands of men in cities all over the world—help a small group of us find our callings in life, find our purposes, and learn to live lives full of significance.

Success is often defined as prosperity, popularity, or profit, while *significance* is defined as important or meaningful. The two may be related, but if they are, they are certainly distant cousins, as I came to find out.

As the class, homework, and reading went on, I realized a couple of things. First, I was way more focused on success than significance, and that had to change. And second, if I was going to pivot toward significance, I needed to spend some time figuring out how God made me.

Prayer and reflection led me to understand a few important truths about myself:

1. I do way better with younger people than with older people. Not proud of it but I cannot lie; old folks' homes are tough for me.
2. If I am going to do something meaningful, then let's get moving to other parts of the world.
3. I am way better at creating a narrative and building a strategy than I am at operating anything.

Bear in mind that these truths are truths for me, not you, or your spouse, or your best friend, or anybody else. A calling is about what makes us tick; it's about what gets us moving sacrificially; it's about what we are willing to risk it all for—just to make it happen. There are no better or worse callings. What is important is that we spend the time figuring out who we are and what we are made to do.

Since I'm on a bit of a roll, I want to reiterate that while our calling in life is about who we are and where we find deep meaning, our unique gifts are likely to be used in a variety of pursuits and take us down a series of different paths throughout our lifetimes. Sometimes, these roads will be planned and easy to understand, but other times, the roads we feel led to take will come out of the blue and be unpredictable. But all the places we go if they are truly in our wheelhouse will embolden and fulfill us—make us happy even when they are hard. Or said another way, you don't pick your passions; your passions pick you.

* * *

Getting together with my son who was a teenager at the time, a few other dads, John and Earl, and their kids who were about the same age, we began to brainstorm about what to do.

Some of the kids had traveled to Belize on a church trip earlier in the summer and lived among the people in a small village who spent much of their day gathering water and trying to purify it so it would not make them sick.

With this as a backdrop, our brainstorming discussion eventually led us to the following vision:

"To rise up a movement of young people who are called to change the world by providing sustainable access to safe drinking water to those in need."

In our case, the proverbial phrase "an idea on the back of a napkin" was actually a bunch of banter we shared while walking around the picnic bench in my backyard. Hands4Others or "H4O" (as a brand as a play on "H2O") for the water component of our mission was born!

While we had great enthusiasm to get after our mission, we lacked the expertise to actually dig a well or build a water system. Wanting to make sure that any funds we raised made a meaningful and lasting impact, we did some research, asked a few friends, and ended up partnering with Water Mission, who in addition to having a four-star Charity Navigator rating (the highest) and being best-in-class engineers were simply some of the most awesome people you could ever meet.

With the water crisis impacting billions of people worldwide, there is an ongoing need for funding, and we agreed to raise the money necessary to bring safe water to a community in northeast Africa.

Starting with a small number of teenage kids leading the way, we shared the reality of the water crisis and our vision mostly in mostly informal gatherings in our family room, sort of like a friends and family round of financing for those of us in the start-up world. And like any start-up, we had to make some changes on the fly.

Initially focusing on the facts, the dire numbers as they relate to those devastated by the lack of safe drinking water, we were missing an emotional connection with our audience. Reading about fundraising, we heard the story about a campaign focused on combating hunger. The organization involved launched three separate campaigns, one with the facts about hunger around the world, the second with facts and a picture of a starving child, and the third with just a picture of a starving child. You guessed it, the campaign with just a picture raised the most money and it wasn't even close. The reason for this is that the facts relating to world hunger, lack of safe water, or sickness are so daunting, so insurmountable that potential investors can feel defeated, like they can't possibly make a difference.

So, we pivoted and began talking about the need to provide water for one child, one family, one village at a time, a vision that people could get their arms around. We showed pictures and shared our vision in a way that left our audience in tears, wanting to help. It worked, and less than a year after that casual meeting in our backyard, we found ourselves in Bondeni, Kenya, proving once again that when we say "yes" to purpose and adventures, big things can things happen and often do.

Africa is far from home, Africa is vast, Africa is awesome! We flew to Nairobi, then traveled via small plane to Kitale—our home base on this trip—then drove through maize fields and dirt roads. Finally, we arrived to see the Bondeni river, which was really more mud than water.

* * *

The scene in the river of kids playing, women washing dishes, cows . . . well, doing what cows do, and people reaching into the water smiling and splashing their faces and filling water buckets with dirty water, all next to one another, was surreal, to say the least.

Moses, our host from Water Mission, is an engaging young man with a big smile and a whole bunch of energy. As we got to know him better, we deemed him the mayor of Kitale, as he seemed to know everyone and could make things happen quickly in a place where things often move slowly. Moses showed us firsthand the engineering aspects of the process of pumping the water from the river, removing the debris and mud, and then sanitizing it to the point that it was as pure as the filtered or bottled water we drink back home.

As is always the case, it is the personal connections we made on this trip that impacted us the most and left us wanting more. At some point during our journey, we visited a neighboring village that had a water system installed a few months prior to our arrival. Moses walked with us to the outskirts of the village where we met a group of ladies who shared their story and the reality of them having to use the vast majority of their modest monthly income for medicine to counteract the effects of drinking bad water. One lady—and I can still picture her to this day—was super tall, had a cast on her arm, and, with great emotion, talked about having worms over a foot long living in her stomach that would reach up to eat food as she was swallowing. She started to cry and told us that now that she had clean water to drink, all her problems were gone. She is healthy and can use her money on better food for her family. We left with tears in our eyes, now understanding the sad truth that many people in this world actually live this way.

We also learned from a principal at a school that before safe drinking water arrived, about 75 percent of the students were absent each day either because they were ill or forced to walk miles to gather the filthy water that was keeping them alive while at the same time slowly killing them from the germs it contained. Since a water treatment system was installed, less than 10 percent of the students were absent on a daily basis. Kids in the community were learning and dreaming of a better life.

I share all this in detail because it's important. It's important for us to know that access to safe water is a key first step to breaking the poverty cycle, and it's important that we do something about it. As the quote attributed to Bono says, "We can be the generation that no longer accepts that an accident of latitude determines whether a child lives or dies. But will we be that generation?" The world is connected today more than ever before, and we can no longer say that we do not know; we can only decide if we care enough to act.

* * *

Celebrations in Kenya are a lengthy affair. Speeches from the chairman of a local theological school, the mayor, and the head of the water district board as well as the heads of numerous committees—all given in the local language, Swahili, and translated to English for our benefit—took up much of the morning. I am not sure of the total attendance, but it felt like most of the three thousand people living in Bondeni were there. Applause followed each speech, and because we were honored guests, people read poems to us and we were offered gifts. This was all quite humbling. After all, we really didn't do that much—we simply helped give them clean water, something that all of us in America take for granted.

The teenagers that got this going were invited to speak, and I think that it was during this time that they began to realize that they could truly make a difference, not later when they were older, but now. In Bondeni, they weren't viewed as teenagers but as capable young people who turned a passion for helping others into tangible action. They were viewed as leaders.

I am convinced that our society, generally speaking, has set the bar way too low in terms of expectations for our kids. At the core, this is what H4O was all about—changing the belief that young people can only do so much. At the core, H4O was about providing a platform that empowers and equips young people to be servant leaders by taking action that benefits others.

Over time, our H4O movement grew, engaging young leaders from all over the world, bringing hundreds of students on vision trips to Mexico, Honduras, Kenya, Indonesia, and Uganda, and helping provide safe drinking water to over two hundred thousand people in fifteen countries. As my wife often says, "You can't dream this stuff up."

After the speeches, the water system was dedicated, and the first taste of clean water poured through the faucets. As is the custom, so we learned, water was sprayed everywhere, and this part of the celebration had officially begun.

With excitement everywhere, lunch was served, and even that was over the top. Maize is a staple in much of Africa while meat, typically chicken and fish, is only served at special occasions. Our friend Moses told us that his family typically eats meat twice a year, at Christmas and Easter, because it is just too expensive. Yet, that day, we were given their very best.

This experience shows what I mean when I say, "We come to help them, and they help us so much more." Those with little in the way of material possession teach us with their selflessness and generosity, and they do so with gratitude and joy, which challenges us who have so much. This is why getting out of our own little bubble is so important. Expanding our playing field allows us to find joy in new and dramatic ways. We are no longer Americans or Africans; rich or poor; black or white. We are all children of God, blessing and loving each other, the way it should be.

While we were eating, the dancing and singing began. I am not a dancer, no way no how, but before we knew it, all of us were up, moving along in this beautiful and spontaneous celebration. Dancing, games, and soccer prevailed. Only when the rain and then the hail came did the party finish, just before dusk. Hugs, tears, and more hugs ended our day in Bondeni, while the memory of what had transpired lives inside us forever.

What had started in Santa Barbara with what I call social banter with a purpose led to the most memorable of experiences in a village clear across the world with people we'd never met before. People who are now connected to us forever, if not in person, then in heart, in memory, in love. It's hard to top this sitting in the office, surfing the web, or following the latest social media sensation.

Mind you, I am not suggesting that we all have to head across the world to make our mark. All of us are wired uniquely and with different passions. Some of the most important acts of service take place in our own communities and neighborhoods with little fanfare or no-tice. The common ground isn't the magnitude of actions we take, but rather that we all get off the couch and move. That we all stop talking and start doing.

As Bob Goff said, "And for me, I've realized that I used to be afraid of failing at the things that really mattered to me, but now I'm more afraid of succeeding at things that don't matter."

Chapter 8

Fun, Fun, Fun

Life is either a daring adventure or nothing at all.
—Helen Keller

In their hit song "Fun, Fun, Fun," the Beach Boys sing about a teenage girl who tricks her father so she can go hot-rodding in his Ford Thunderbird. Sounds like a fairly common teenage stunt. Heck, I did much worse—no details forthcoming.

Everybody wants to have fun, that we can all agree on, and fun is found in different ways for different people during different seasons in our lives.

But where does helping others first come into play? Sometimes I think people view the responsibility that comes with a life of service as a buzzkill where all the excitement dies. Where cruising in a convertible is frowned upon or not allowed. Well, I can say from experience that nothing is further from the truth.

* * *

As H4O grew, we began to expand the size of our groups and the number of vision trips we took each summer. The ages of the kids on these trips varied from about twelve years old to eighteen years old, mostly high school kids with a few junior high students on the younger end and a handful of college students on the older side of things.

Each year, we took kids from different schools, different cities, and different ethnic and socioeconomic backgrounds. Being in school once a long time ago and being a parent, I am not naïve about the reality of different cliques: the cool kids, the jocks, and the nerds, to name a few. (OK, the "nerds" is old school, but you know what I mean). But none of these cliques formed on these trips. No social media, no fancy clothes, no status: just a group of young people, all with their insecurities and challenges, joining together to do something bigger than themselves.

Part of my joy on these trips is listening to the kids talk—not text, not post, just talk. I still remember this one night.

It was late after a long day, all of us filthy, loaded with tons of suntan lotion and bug spray, sort of soaking in our last moments in the village where we had worked and played all day. I heard a couple of the older girls talking:

"I wish I could live here; life is simpler here without all the drama."

"Yeah, me too. Home is just so busy, so complicated."

While none of us moved to Honduras, their conversation does highlight an interesting point. Fun comes in all shapes and sizes, and sometimes, the shapes and sizes are not always what we think.

* * *

Every vision trip is special. There is no "best" trip, and no trips are ever the same. They all take on a life of their own. The work we do is serious and difficult. Water systems are heavy—really heavy. Cement for latrines is also heavy, really heavy. Digging trenches for piping with shovels and pitchforks is painful and time consuming. Doing all this in ninety-degree weather with ninety-degree humidity makes it even more demanding. But our kids do the work without complaining, with smiles on their faces and while bonding with other kids of all ages in the local communities. It is special and amazing to watch.

I like to call the philosophy behind these trips "chaos with a purpose," which means that we have a plan and an itinerary, but we also allow for spontaneity; and if I am honest, it is often these unscripted moments that are the most memorable. Some of these moments are sad or gnarly—like the day we built a latrine for a widow with five kids. Her husband had been a drunk who had gotten killed in a bar fight, leaving her with all the kids to raise on her own. She kept crying and thanking us. We thought for building her a latrine, but it turns out that she was thanking us for the Polaroid pictures of her and her family that we printed and gave to her. One of the locals explained that these were the first time she'd ever had pictures of her children.

Then there was the time when a little boy, about five years old and wearing a Superman shirt, followed us around the village all day holding hands interchangeably with every girl on our trip. At the end of the day, when he realized that we were leaving, he just lost it, breaking down in tears and holding onto the girls. Most of us were in tears as well, and it took us three false starts before we actually left, as we got out of our van several times to hold him tight just one more time.

Of course, some moments are just plain ridiculous.

Picture hopping in a couple of outrigger canoes at dusk to go and visit an island off the coast so small that you could literally throw a baseball over it. Then picture returning to the mainland at night through a canal lit by burning logs—a scene right out of *Pirates of the Caribbean* where we were led out of a beachside village by a couple of guys on horseback who warned us to be careful of the crocodiles.

Or think about Bennett, twelve years old and the youngest trip participant that year, begging me to allow him to get on the roof of our van with the older kids while riding through a jungle on the way to a village. I conceded and said yes—but with the stipulation that if he fell off and broke his arm or leg, I was leaving him behind. No way I was bringing him home with a cast and experiencing his mom's wrath. (This is where we coined the phrase, "What happens in Honduras stays in Honduras.")

Then, there was the year of the coffee—when the kids went from not being coffee drinkers to drinking coffee with the locals, then to buying coffee in bulk and bringing it back to the States and turning it into a social business and a "coffee4water" campaign. All the coffee bags made for an interesting trip through security and customs on the way home, but we made it and ended up raising funds to help install another water system.

And who could forget the time Bryn and Olivia were playing alongside a bunch of cows with the local kids? They were splashing and jumping about in the river of mud created by an incessant afternoon rainstorm only to realize that they weren't playing in mud.

I could keep going forever, but you get the idea: magic happens, and memories are created when we get out of our comfort zone.

My favorite tradition on every trip happens at the end of the day. We could be staying in a hotel as our home base or in a church, school, or other enclosure in a village way out in the middle of nowhere. Regardless, every evening, we share our best and worst experiences of the day. Sometimes the stories are silly, sometimes they are serious, but in each case, they are something different from the norm, something meaningful and far beyond the scope of life back home. And the memories stick, and the lessons learned carry on. Even after returning home, where we slip back into our routines, our more comfortable lives, and forget how much of the world actually lives, the truth is none of us can ever unsee what we've seen. We come back forever changed, in a good way, a lasting way.

* * *

One of these trips brought us to a small, remote village in Honduras where we were tasked with building a latrine for a poor family. By American standards, all the families in this community were poor, but this particular family really broke our hearts. They had a number of kids who were absolutely adorable, and we all fell in love with a little girl named Maya. Maya was eight years old, although she looked much younger than her age from malnourishment.

During the day, we noticed that she had marks all over her neck. When we asked how she got them, we were told that they were from bats who flew into her makeshift house during the night and bit her and her siblings.

Their house consisted of two rooms, dirt floors, and straw walls. It was situated right against a steep hill, meaning that in the rainy season, mud would flow off the hill underneath the straw walls and turn the house into a muddy mess. Maya and her family would literally get out of bed and step into puddles of mud.

By the end of the day, we finished building the latrine, which was far nicer than their house and gave them their first chance to avoid the great outdoors when going to the bathroom. By then, we had completely fallen in love with Maya and her entire family.

Getting back to our hotel, we could not shake the images of their house and what their lives would be like during the rainy season; and that night, a couple of other dads on the trip and I decided that we were going to build Maya and her family a new home. Great idea. Pure hearts. Now, what do we do next?

In general, home building was not a strong suit for any of us, least of all me. Doing so in a foreign country like Honduras seemed a fairly insurmountable obstacle. So, we approached our host, Hector, the in-country director for Water Mission.

He explained to us how things work in Honduras. First, we needed to be very careful how the title on the home was held to make sure the family was secure and able to stay there, since the legal system in Honduras is not always on the up and up. Second, we agreed that building the home had to be done outside the purview of Water Mission or Hands4Others since both of our stated missions dealt with water and not housing. Third, we needed to be patient. Things take time in Honduras.

A couple of quick thoughts about this whole idea:

1. I do not want to overstate our generosity. Building a cinder block home in Honduras is not like building a home in the United States. The total cost was about $4,000.

2. We also understood that we could not build a home for every poor family we met along the way and that for Water Mission or H4O to do so would result in us being a "jack of all trades and master of none" and ultimately dilute, not increase, our impact. We were simply following what we felt God put on our hearts. It was not efficient, strategic, or tactical, all the things I usually think about. It was all about heart, and I am OK with that—at least on occasion.

The risk of all these heart-led, spur-of-the-moment ideas is that the passion tends to fade over time, and the more difficult the task, the less likely we follow through. It is kind of like when we see something in the store and just have to have it, but if we don't buy it, we get home and realize we really didn't need to have it after all and move on to the next thing. It is the reason why car salesmen or saleswomen try to close the deal before you leave the lot and why charity functions ask for money at the event, in the moment. They understand that when we get home, we tend to lose our stoke and are less likely to commit. In this case, the cure for us fading on our big idea was to carry a picture of Maya as a reminder of what was at stake.

Returning home, Hector dealt with the title. We sent the money, and two years after we met Maya, we returned to find a small, simple, but beautiful home with cement floors and cinder block walls. Arriving in a group with some familiar faces and some new ones as well, we were greeted by the father, who was thankful but a bit embarrassed, the mother, who kept hugging us and crying, and the kids (now plus one more), who were a bit shy, probably not remembering who we were.

Funny how lime green paint is a cure for shyness. Our task for the afternoon—if you could call it that—was to paint this new house and lime green was the color of choice. So, first carefully and then without reserve we painted the house . . . and each other. Maya was bigger now, not as easily held but still adorable, and the joy, laughter, and gratitude from her and her entire family made for one of those special days that remind us that a life lived for others may be hard, but it is also fun, fun, fun.

* * *

While fun is often found when we are out of our comfort zone, it is not limited to just those times in which we are serving others in a grand way. I remember my friend and spiritual mentor, Pastor Ricky Ryan, always reminding me that God created surfing (his favorite) and skiing and fly-fishing (my favorites) so that we can enjoy all that life has to offer.

For some time, I've hosted an annual guys' ski trip to Colorado. Some of my friends are regulars or semiregulars on these trips, while others have just shown up once. Being a bit of a last-minute guy, I have always allowed my intuition or circumstances to bring the right people on the right trip and try to have a blend of guys at different stages of life. There is not meant to be any exclusivity to the group other than lodging constraints, and hey, if you have not been invited thus far—make me an offer.

There is also not much of a scheduled agenda on these trips. Once again, I'm spontaneous at times, and the goal (if there is one) is to support one another and share our blessings and trials all in the midst of crazy, fun times.

A few years back, I remember our pack of six skiers and two snow-boarders, led by Ryan wearing a bright orange ski parka, taking turns shredding all over the mountain. Great food for dinner followed by banter around the fire pit eventually led to the collective decision to engage in some friendly nighttime saucer races. We all loved going down the hill, but not so much walking back up, so we ultimately got in the car and drove up to the top of the mountain, where we all strapped on our skis and took a few turns down the moonlit slopes.

But in the midst of breaking a few rules (which I am quite sure we did) and insane fun (which we certainly had), we also spent a fair amount of time sharing and praying for one another. There is something about being away in a retreat-like setting that creates a safe environment where we can all be vulnerable and honest with one another.

This particular year, like most years, we went to church on Sunday at the top of Beaver Creek Mountain, where Pastor Tommy held a short service after lunch right on the ski slopes. Singing out loud in your ski gear while gazing upon the Gore Mountain Range with your bros and other folks from around the world is pretty darn cool.

In the most basic sense, it appears that working hard with a bunch of kids in the jungle of Honduras and night skiing with my friends have little in common. One is all about service and helping others while the other is pretty much about play and helping myself to a good time. But on a deeper level, the two share some common threads, and they both play an important role in a life that is effective, fun, and full of joy. Adventure and purpose take on different forms, and while I am quite sure that a life full of giving, not getting, is the recipe for the biggest piece of the pie, we do need to find time to recharge, share, and grow. We have to have a community around us, and we must be strong in body, soul, mind, and spirit to do our best work.

Anybody up for some fun?

Chapter 9

Give Me Your Eyes

Give me Your love for humanity
Give me Your arms for the broken-hearted
The ones that are far beyond my reach
Give me Your heart for the ones forgotten
Give me Your eyes so I can see
—Brandon Heath

The words to "Give Me Your Eyes," the award-winning song written and sung by my friend Brandon Heath, really speak into this idea of seeing others how God sees all of us, full of love, compassion, and empathy. The lyrics challenge us to be aware of what others are going through, to listen, observe, and help. I am afraid that far too often, when we greet somebody and ask "How's it going?" or "How are you doing?," we don't really mean what we say, and we don't really care—it's just another way to say hello.

Even more often, when we hear about someone else's suffering, our attention span is short. They get a few moments of our thoughts, and then it's right back to "population me."

* * *

Way back when my kids were little, we had a semiregular meeting with a middle-aged lady outside of Baskin-Robbins. Now my kids are into the trendier ice creams, such as McConnell's or Rori's, but for years I would steer them to Baskin-Robbins, my favorite, which is one of the few perks of being the family financier.

She tried hard to keep herself together and looked good compared with many of the people living "on the street," but you could just tell she was homeless. We sort of adopted her and gave her some food or money each time we saw her and eventually began to have conversations. She was always alone, had it together mentally, and didn't appear to be under the influence, which made the whole thing even more heartbreaking. At one point, we learned her story, which, as expected, was sad—lousy parents, no safety net, willing to work but without many sought-after skills. Like I said, super sad.

One night, she shared the hardest part of not having a home. Surprisingly, it wasn't what we thought. It wasn't the lack of food or shelter or the fear of violence; it was loneliness and the shame she felt as people avoided her and refused to make eye contact.

* * *

Many years later, Vicki and I were strolling back to our hotel in the town of Jackson, Wyoming. We were on a short getaway to one of the world's most beautiful places in late fall and after a morning hike and photo op in front of the Tetons had stopped in town to pick up some souvenirs and snacks. As we beelined for the hotel and a shower and some rest, we passed a young man who was trying to get our attention. Mostly oblivious to our surroundings and not all that interested in what he wanted, we kept moving until we were about a half a block or so past him, when we heard him say, "Never mind, have a nice day."

For some reason, the Baskin-Robbins lady came to my head, so we stopped, walked back, and asked him what was happening. He was a big guy, a bit disheveled, wearing camouflage gear and carrying a large backpack—not that out of place for the town of Jackson, which attracts the rugged outdoor crowd. He did not appear to be homeless but also did not appear to be flush or a resident of local lodging.

We began to chat and eventually he just broke down, sharing through the tears how he was a hunting guide in a neighboring town who worked up here in the fall, sending money back home to Alabama where his family lived, and how he got word that his wife had died suddenly. Now he just needed some extra money to hop on a bus and get home to his kids. He explained that he was staying at a local church that offered him shelter and some food but was struggling to find anyone to lend him an ear, let alone help him.

Trying to keep a generous heart but also programmed to be a bit skeptical of money requests, we asked him a few questions in a sort of mild cross-examination. He told us where the local bus stop was located, showed us his ID and pictures of his family, and offered to pull up the local news story about his wife on our phone. At that point, my heart said, "*Drew—stop—enough.*" Reading my mind, Vicki asked, "How much do you need?" He showed us his stash, which was about $140, explaining he needed a total of $260 to get all the way home. We pulled out our wallet, which like most people's today is long on plastic but short on cash. Fortunately, we had about $150 on us, which we gave to him, figuring that should get him home and some food on the way.

He was either Oscar worthy or the real deal and just cried and hugged us, thanking us and promising that he was telling the truth. We got his kid's names, held hands, and prayed over him as people passed us by, oblivious to what was happening, just like we were a few minutes before we stopped and listened. Give me Your arms for the broken-hearted.

* * *

I am pretty sure that the Zulu people get it right with their standard greeting "*Sawubona*," which means "I see you, I really see you," as do the words to the Monk & Neagle song "The Twenty-First Time," which reminds us that the people who have it hard, that society dismisses at times, are real people with their own stories, people who long for love and dignity, just like the rest of us. The words encourage us to slow down and hear them, to cultivate a heart for them that we should have, the heart for them that God wants us to have.

* * *

I get exhausted just thinking about the lives of pastors and other spiritual leaders. Their lives are nonstop, combining the role of senior management (leading their respective organizations) and emergency room doctor (always on call). As much as their jobs seem different from those of us who work in the "regular" world, they also face some of the marketplace pressures in the sense that many of the people who come to listen on Sundays (or these days watch online) expect to be inspired; otherwise, they can quickly move on to a different church where the pastor has a cooler vibe or more charisma.

Preparing sermons, managing people, and then being available when crisis hits is a 24/7 endeavor and one that requires a great deal of compassion, love, wisdom, and stamina. As someone who is close friends with a handful of pastors, I have always encouraged them to find time to rest, turn off their phones, and be with their wives and families. To run this kind of race effectively, they need to exhale and refresh on occasion.

Pastor Tommy and Pastor Bret, who head up our church in Santa Barbara, run hard, promote excellence, and combine a servant heart with the ability to lead and execute at the highest level. In my view, they are two of the most awesome people out there.

Sometimes they refresh together, taking their wives and getting away to relax, dream, and hang out. A few years back, they took a couple of days off and headed up to Lake Arrowhead, a pristine place up in the Southern California mountains where they could be among nature, share their hearts, and feel close to God.

Turns out, even on retreats, crisis follows these guys. One morning in the midst of the stillness of a tranquil setting, they heard the cries of a woman: "Help me! Please help!" The cries were loud and desperate, repeated over and over again.

In the mountains, sound travels in weird ways, bouncing off the hillsides with echoes, making it difficult to figure out exactly where it's coming from. The guys began to run down the sloping hillside toward the lake, frantically trying to figure out the location of the screams. They finally ended up a ways down the hill, staring up at a balcony on the back of a house held up by stilts, the way homes on steep hills are usually secured to offer outdoor living and a view.

There, they found the source of the noise: a young lady, lying face down on the balcony, reaching under the railing and holding on to the wrists of a young man who was dangling feetfirst over the side.

It was too far of a drop for them to catch the guy; trying to do so would just kill or injure everyone. So, they quickly ran up the hill, entered the house through the unlocked door, and scampered through the hallways and onto the balcony, where they both dove, each of them grabbing one of guy's wrists.

Now that she could let go, the girl fell back on the deck, overwhelmed, exhausted, and crying. The guy struggled a bit, acting in a way that made it seem like he wasn't sure if he wanted to be rescued. Getting some leverage, Pastor Bret, who is a big dude, finally reached over, grabbed him by his pants, and pulled him over the balcony, where they all lay in a heap, sweating and full of adrenaline.

Patiently, they began to calm down both the guy and girl and talk them off the ledge—no pun intended. Amid lots of tears, some raw emotion, and a few swear words, the couple began to open up and admit that their relationship was volatile: too much partying, scream fights, breakups (followed by makeups), and now, a moment in which he wasn't sure he wanted to live without her.

At some point, as the four of them sat in a circle talking, the couple learned that both Tommy and Bret are pastors, which really wrecked their world in a good way, "Wow, I guess God is really saying something when He sends a couple of pastors to save me," said the dude who minutes before was dangling from the balcony. Funny how even those who are so far away from thinking about God tend to want Him near when the going gets tough. Bret and Tommy prayed for them, local help arrived, and they kept in touch via text for a while—all in a day's work, even on vacation.

Hours after the "rescue" began, the guys headed back up the hill and observed a man sitting on his balcony next door watching the whole thing, which begs the question: Why did no one else help? Tommy, Bret, and their wives were blocks away from the scene. There is no possible way this guy who was right next to this couple's house couldn't hear the screams. There was no way anyone remotely close to their house could miss the cries for help. Yet, no one else showed up.

I hate to bring cynicism into my writings, but I can't help but think that many people chicken out and run away when the going gets tough; or, as one of my friends says, "Many people in this world suffer from the same affliction: lack of spine." I believe that those who complain the most rarely chip in and that those who scream the loudest usually have the least to say. It is the unsung people who don't draw attention to themselves or their actions that usually do the most for others and are life's true heroes. In this case, a couple of these unsung folks saved some stranger's life.

* * *

I was swapping stories with my friend Rick, like guys like to do, and he shared with me about the time he and a buddy were traveling in China and met the pastor of an underground church in a poor, rural area, the kind of place where tourists never go and is as different from the crowded cities of Beijing and Shanghai as a place could possibly be. The meeting took place like too many meetings are forced to take place in much of the world: in a hush-hush manner so "Big Brother" doesn't see.

The pastor explained that the whole church was praying for access to some medicine needed to heal a woman in the church who was dying without it. When Rick asked how much the medicine cost, the pastor told him $94. Shocked that the need could be met for such a small sum of money, Rick and his friend went into their wallets and each of them gave the pastor $47, at which point the pastor started yelling in excitement over the miracle that God had performed.

Rick, being a humble guy, tried to downplay the whole thing by reminding him that it was no big deal; it was only $94. The pastor responded, "You do not understand. We have not seen someone from the West in over ten years. Every day, we pray for God to provide us with this medicine even though we know we could never get the money to afford it on our own. We even pray as a church all night for God to help our sister who is sick. Now, here, today, in the middle of a small village in China, two men from America show up with the money; this is truly a miracle!"

As they continued to chat, the pastor let Rick know that about two hundred people attended his church. Rick, being a bit curious about the all-night prayer session since we do not see too many of those in the US, asked the pastor how many people in the church show up to pray all night. The pastor looked at him, puzzled, and said, "Two hundred"—like, of course the whole church shows up; what kind of silly question is that?

Give me Your eyes to see the beauty of two hundred people willing to stay up all night praying because they care. Give me Your eyes to see those clear across the world who don't have $94 and can't fathom a way to get it. Give me Your heart so I do something for the forgotten.

* * *

Since we were swapping stories, I told Rick about the time I found myself in a small rural village in central Kenya.

This village was a four-hour drive from the town where we were staying. After four hours of winding roads filled with potholes, hailstorms, and maize fields, we arrived (a bit carsick) at our destination to the excitement of children greeting us with "*Musongo, Musongo*," which means "white person, white person" in Swahili. Many of the people, especially the children living in these remote destinations, have rarely if ever seen a white person, and our arrival is often met with great excitement and anticipation.

As I got out of the car to giggles and high fives and looked through the sea of humanity in front of me, I saw in the background a familiar face calling my name. It took me a minute to place him, and then I remembered that it was a man named Peter. Peter and I had met a couple of years before and spent one day together. He was a linguist we'd used to translate Swahili into English and vice versa.

On this day, Peter invited us over to his house for coffee or tea, and as we walked through the village to his modest house with dirt floors and walls made of mud and straw, we learned that Peter had left Kitale, the bigger town where we were staying and the town where he had lived when we first met him, for this remote village to work on his translation business and look to help improve the lives of people in the village.

Our day changed when I innocently asked Peter about his family. He had a young son we had bonded with a few years back, and I wanted to know how he was doing. But when I asked about his son, Peter's body and face just dropped. He became super emotional, took a few minutes to gather himself, then let us know that he knew when he moved to this rural village that he was giving up some of the comforts he was used to having, such as a cement floor and electricity. He knew he was moving further away from the "city" but felt like he and his family could really help and serve others who were less fortunate by moving here. He shared that when his son got sick, he tried to get down the mountain to medical care in Kitale where he used to live, but by the time they got to the hospital, his son had passed away.

Sometimes when we hear about tragedy from afar, it's hard to get overwhelmed. It just isn't that real or impacts us in a personal way. But this was *right* in front of me, and having kids myself, I couldn't help but weep for my friend and his loss.

I have thought about Peter a fair amount over the years and shared his story as one of sacrifice and hardship in trying to do the right thing. Most people who have listened felt like I do, sympathetic and sad, but some have expressed frustration that perhaps Peter was reckless with his son's life in pursuit of some crazy personal dream. At first, I was shocked and even angry at these observations, but as my heart and emotions quieted down, I realized this tension between risk and security is real and relevant, especially when it comes to our kids.

In my head, I sorted this out into two buckets: action and motive. In Peter's case, moving to rural Kenya is like someone in America moving from the city to a farm or ranch, leaving the rat race for a mellow life and understanding that by doing so, they are giving up some modern amenities, including robust healthcare close by. I don't see any of this as reckless, but rather a lifestyle decision that, like all decisions, has pluses and minuses. Tragic for sure, but not because Peter did something wrong.

Recently, I was reading a magazine that focused on outdoor pursuits. There were two articles back-to-back. The first was about a young man who decided he was supposed to go help a group of people isolated and known for their violent behavior against outsiders. When he was killed doing so, the article viewed his decision as naïve and foolish. The next article talked about a group of friends who were always pushing the envelope and one winter tried a hike that no one had done before. They never returned, leaving behind family and friends. In this case, their actions were glorified: "They died doing what they loved."

I suppose we could debate the wisdom of both decisions, but as far as motives go, I think the articles got them backward. Peter, as well as the young man in the first article, found tragedy while trying to help someone else, whereas the group of guys in the second article found tragedy trying to do something for themselves. The first is selfless and the second is in some ways selfish.

I am not picking on the guys who died hiking. My heart is sad for them and their loved ones. Nor am I saying that we shouldn't push our limits trying the double black diamond ski run or Class 4 rapid—I'm just making the point that motives matter. They show the condition of our hearts.

* * *

Later, I told Rick about the time on one of our trips to Africa during which I was traveling around the Lake Victoria region of Uganda.

Lake Victoria is one of the largest freshwater lakes in the world (over twenty-six thousand square miles) and a beautiful part of the world. As I sat in the small outrigger canoe going from one remote fishing village to another, I couldn't help but think about this being an area where expensive homes and resorts should cover the shorelines, with sailboats, Jet Skis, and other water sports having plenty of room to coexist.

While I am sure there are many reasons why this hasn't happened, I know that one of them is because the bilharzia parasite lives in the lake. I am not trying to dazzle you with my knowledge of the African continent or the dangerous bugs of the world; I just happened to be in the area and thus learned about this little parasite that has a dominant effect on the lives of those living in and around the lake. Not easily seen by the naked eye, the bilharzia parasite is dangerous and can make us really sick. It is often carried by snails around the shoreline, thus making the water dangerous to swim in, yet let alone drink. So, the area that could be like a Ugandan version of Lake Tahoe is instead poor and desolate in places, with a sprinkling of villages dotting the lake, all trying to survive through fishing in what we back home would call a primitive manner.

One day, I was visiting one of these villages and was struck by the irony of seeing this beautiful land and water combination—the harbors that could surely be built and flourish—and the sad reality that many people in this village would die, literally die, because they didn't have safe water to drink.

Why? How can this be? Is it because those of us with the resources are "weak sauce," as friends and I like to call each other when we wimp out from doing something difficult and challenging? Is it because we don't care enough? The answer is probably more complex, but in a way, I think yes.

In the fast-paced life that many of us live, it is easy to become callous or indifferent to the suffering of others. "Hey, I got my own problems." Yes, that is true, we all have our stuff that needs fixing. But, in my experience, the best way to get over our personal trials is to take our eyes off ourselves and look outward at those around us. To see the homeless lady, the widow, or the stranger in trouble and do something, even something small, to make their lives better. To step out even when it is risky and help someone in need.

Try it and see what happens!

Give me Your eyes.

Chapter 10

Just Say Yes

Your life has been intentionally designed by
God to have a uniquely significant and eternal
impact on the world around you.
—Tony Dungy

I heard a story a while back about Albert Einstein traveling on a train. When the train conductor got to his seat to punch his ticket, Einstein went to take it from his shirt pocket. When it wasn't there, he checked his jacket pockets, then his pants pockets, then on the seat where he was sitting. Sensing that he was struggling to find it, the train conductor said, "Mr. Einstein, I know who you are and surely know that you have purchased a ticket, so please don't worry about it, it is fine."

Walking toward the end of that particular car, the conductor looked back before walking through the door to the next compartment only to see the great Albert Einstein on all fours, frantically searching under his chair, obviously looking for his ticket. Hustling back up the aisle, the conductor reminded Einstein, "Sir, as I said, I know who you are, and surely the conductor on the next train you take will know who you are. Please don't worry about it. It is an honor to have you on my train."

Looking up, still on his knees, Albert Einstein replied, "Yes, I appreciate the fact that you know who I am. I too know who I am; what I don't know is where I am going."

If we think about it, isn't that what most of us, maybe even all of us, think about more than anything else? Where are we going, and what happens when we die? And what should my life on this earth look like? What does the future hold, and how can I find the greatest joy and fulfillment while I am alive?

All of the major religions or philosophies, even the more obscure or fringe followings, attempt to address these two basic questions in one form or another.

The reality is just as Albert Einstein was searching for his train ticket, we are all searching for something, some kind of meaning. My favorite song from the band Chicago, "(I've Been) Searchin' So Long," speaks into this theme, encouraging us to find an answer to life's meaning.

A few years back on my birthday after a workout with my family, we wandered into a local smoothie shop to get some healthy nourishment and this song by Chicago was actually playing as we were ordering. I kind of viewed it as a mini-blessing, a minor gift to top off what had already been a nice morning with my wife and kids.

I'm a bit of a wanderer in stores and like to check out what is going on, and in this case, I ended up taking a look at the bulletin board, which provides local businesses and causes a place to advertise whatever it is they are doing. Here are just a few of the flyers I saw on that day:

- "Mastering Life, Love, and Financial Well-Being: Making the Big Leap to Your Highest Potential"
- "Introduction to Clairvoyant Healing"
- "Love"
- "Healing and Meditation"
- "Learn to Transform Your Relationship"

All the while, I was listening to Peter Cetera and the rest of the band sing the words to "(I've Been) Searchin' So Long." It was kind of a quirky moment where the words to a song matched perfectly with what I was doing and observing.

While these self-help opportunities might be helpful in some ways, I do wonder why when Jesus offers this free gift of grace, love, and forgiveness that our churches don't have a line out the door to get in. I think at the end of the day, it is at least in part because we mess up the message. Instead of sharing what we are for, we harp on what we are against. To quote Toula's father, Gus Portokalos, a main character in the hilarious movie *My Big Fat Greek Wedding*, we become like a dry piece of toast.

"Don't watch this show. Don't listen to that type of music. You can't hang with those people—they don't think or live the way we do. We don't shop there—I don't like what they stand for. Don't live in that neighborhood—it isn't safe. Oh, we don't travel to that part of the world. It is way too dangerous." While I am certainly not advocating for a life without boundaries or principles, I do think it's hard to inspire people when we're living a life of scarcity, worried about all the things that can go wrong. It's far more inspiring to live a life of abundance, sharing all the things that we are for, all the things that can go right.

* * *

Our family's first foray into the world of mission trips was an annual trip with our church to Mexico in early December. We passed out Christmas presents, served a lunch of hot dogs and cookies at a sister church in Ensenada, and visited other churches in small villages as well as a school for deaf children, where we brought supplies for the teachers and students.

One year, we showed up at the deaf school only to encounter a couple hundred Harley-Davidson motorcycles and their riders, who unbeknownst to us were generous supporters of the school. Watching these big and somewhat intimidating guys brought to tears by the kids at the school and then ask us for prayer is another one of the unexpected ways our lives are changed when we say "yes." If you can, picture the image of us arriving in our church van, more than a bit nervous and intimidated by the scene, only to end up with our heads bowed, holding hands and praying with a bunch of dudes who live lives about as different from me and my family as they could possibly be.

Another time, we gathered with the pastor in El Zorrillo, a small town outside Ensenada, and helped his wife heat water on the stove one teakettle at a time, making sure the temperature was just right, then poured it into a small plastic tub (the kind you get at Kmart or the dollar store for ninety-nine cents) until it was full and ready to bathe their infant daughter. The process took about an hour and looked quite a bit different from turning on a faucet and enjoying the long, hot showers or baths we are used to at home.

Driving back to Santa Barbara, we had a long and emotional discussion about the pastor's life and the poverty that all of those living in El Zorrillo face, but we also talked about how they found joy and hope from the love of Jesus. This was one of those teachable moments in which I was able to share with my kids that they should not feel guilty about the comforts they enjoy, but they should do something purposeful with their lives. They should use their blessings to make the world a better place.

I still remember the first time we took our youngest child, Dani, to Mexico when she was three years old. She is the fairest of our children, and her blond, almost white hair and big blue eyes were so distinct and different that all the local kids wanted to touch her and hold her hand. We still have pictures framed of her and the local kids from a number of our trips over the years, always with a stark contrast in physical appearance, but never a contrast of heart. Smiles and laughter are contagious, and, in this way, kids get it right far more often than us adults.

Some of our friends and peers thought we were crazy to bring her at three years old on a trip like this. We thought we'd be crazy not to bring her. I admit I am an adventurous traveler and think that the perceived or stated risk of travel is usually overhyped, and that generally things are much safer than those in charge lead us to believe. But seriously, if we are going to raise the next generation of leaders in a way that moves things forward, not backward, we can't do it by sitting on the couch and watching someone else do it. We need to regulate our protective nature as parents and avoid sheltering our kids. We need to live the life we want our children to lead, and we need to take them with us.

* * *

If the dictionary had a picture for positivity, high energy, or encouragement, I am pretty sure that picture would be of Ricky Ryan. Ricky grew up in Orange County, a surf rat, and said yes when Chuck Smith invited him to his growing tent church called Calvary Chapel in the 1960s. At a time when more traditional churches turned away the grungy surf crowd, Pastor Chuck invited them in and started a revolution with Ricky Ryan right in the middle of it.

Pastor Ricky said yes when Jesus came knocking, said yes to becoming a pastor, said yes when he started a church in Maui, and yet yes again when he was asked to come to Santa Barbara and start a church here. Ricky said yes and let's go when he felt led to move the church from downtown Santa Barbara to an empty warehouse next to the water treatment (fancy word for sewage) plant, then said yes and amen to doing Easter service right in the middle of Santa Barbara in the sunken garden adjacent to our historic courthouse, a tradition that continues to this day, regularly serving over four thousand people on Easter Sunday.

- *Want to start a church? Yes. Go!*
- *Want to launch a ministry? Yes. How can I help?*
- *Want to take a risk for God? Yes. You better.*

Lots of yeses in the life of Ricky Ryan, but it is the yes from March 14, 2010, that sets Ricky apart and elevates him to the status of a great servant leader.

On that Sunday morning in 2010, Ricky Ryan let a packed congregation know that he was stepping down as the senior pastor of Calvary Chapel Santa Barbara. He didn't do it because of some scandal or problem. He did it because he listened and felt like God said it was time. No one—I mean no one—would have ever asked Ricky to leave. He was bigger than life; heck, God used Ricky to build His church in this town. Ricky was loved, but as he reminded us all that morning amid the tears, "It is not Ricky's church; it is God's church."

In his book *What Makes a Leader Great,* Russ Crosson highlights the fact that a great leader leads to replace him or herself. In other words, "It's not about us. It's about those who come after us." Not easy if we are sold on the fact that our worth is found by elevating our own status or receiving more and more praise.

It takes a strong leader, a servant leader, a humble leader, to step aside before they're asked. Far too often, it is the other way around, where leaders stay and stay and stay until they are asked to leave or forced to leave.

And it's not like Ricky's done leading. He is just doing so back in Maui where it all began, with a great big hug and a bunch of surfboards waiting for all of us who visit.

* * *

If humility is the greatest virtue, then pride is the most destructive of all our vices. It is pride that causes men and women to fail and is particularly dangerous for those of us doing "good" in the world. As the American novelist Nathaniel Hawthorne wrote, "Benevolence is the twin of pride," meaning that helping others can quickly become more about what we get instead of the actual service itself. Oswald Chambers expands on this point in a different way when he says, "If our devotion is to the cause of humanity, we will be quickly defeated and broken-hearted, since we will often be confronted with a great deal of ingratitude from other people. But if we are motivated by our love for God, no amount of ingratitude will be able to hinder us from serving one another."

I once was asked by a college student how I knew when to say "yes" and how I knew when to say "no." My short answer was to "say no more than you say yes, but when you say yes, mean it!" To clarify, I think most of us should say "yes" a whole lot more than we do, but I also think there is a discipline to picking the assignments for which we have passion, energy, and stamina. There is a constructive benefit to not running aimlessly with frenetic energy from one thing to the next as well as knowing when our time is up.

Ricky Ryan understands this: he knew when to say "yes" and lead, and he knew when to say "yes" and leave. He lives for his God. That's enough for him. I hope it is enough for me.

Chapter 11

Half-Full or Half-Empty?

When is the last time you did something for the first time?
—John Maxwell

Technically, to the letter, the answer is yes, the glass is both half-full and half-empty. But in real life, we view this proverbial phrase one of two ways. Half-empty kind of reminds me of Eeyore from the classic Winnie-the-Pooh series, like we are stuck in a worldview of pessimism, focused on the problems of life more than the solutions. Half-full reminds me of a Vince Vaughn and Owen Wilson movie, like the blender scene in *The Internship*. Check it out if you have not seen it and you will know what I mean. Half-full is about endless possibilities. It is full of hope and action.

Imagine a life like the one John Maxwell calls us to lead, a life full of new stuff, new ideas, new adventures, new ways to make our mark in the world. Sounds a lot more fun, a lot more full than "same ol', same ol'."

* * *

A number of years ago, I was on a church trip and found myself in central Mexico. Toward the end of the trip, one of the ladies who was leading the trip mentioned that she was sad that this year the church would not be able to give their usual gift to the pastors at the local churches.

OK, I'll bite, I thought. "Why not?"

"Well, we are in the process of setting up a new 501(c)(3) for this ministry, and until it is established, there is no money available for them."

"Why not just use some of the money in the mission's budget?"

"We would, but there's no money in the mission's budget for this ministry."

"Why not just get a few folks to donate the money?"

"We thought of that, but it won't work because if the gifts are earmarked for this ministry, the IRS will not allow for a tax deduction."

"Hmm . . . how much money are we talking about here?"

"Well, we have five pastors we support, and each year we give them a gift of $100, so the total is $500."

Wait a minute, I thought. *We are talking about $500 to bless pastors who are living in houses smaller than the size of many people's closets back home, and we can't get donations because there is no tax write-off? Seriously?*

I tend to carry some cash with me when I travel abroad, figuring cash is the best thing to have if there is trouble. I am not being a hotshot here, but I went into my travel bag and handed her five $100 bills. She looked at me kind of inquisitively and reminded me that I wouldn't get a write-off. *Ahhhhhh!* I wanted to yell. *I know it is 500 dollars, not 5 million dollars! Who cares?*

First, let me say that I am not advocating that any of us skirt IRS rules when dealing with donations. Obviously, being squeaky clean in this way matters a great deal. Hard to offer influence and advocate for others if our own house isn't in order.

Second, it is wise and prudent to make charitable donations in a tax-efficient manner. I certainly do this. But we were talking about a relatively small amount of money here, and I just don't think we show the love of Jesus or change the world when we major in the minors.

Half-full or half-empty? Abundance or scarcity? The answer matters and the stakes are high.

It matters because when we live with a scarcity point of view, it is easy to start pulling back from doing, from helping, from serving.

Case in point: I remember back to the 2008–2009 financial crises, during which some teenagers I knew called a rich guy asking him for a donation to a local charity. The man responded by saying something like this: "Sorry, fellows, not right now—things are tight. The markets are lousy." OK, I get it, except they were asking for $50, and he was turning them down while sitting in his private plane on his way to his ski chalet.

Let us remember what God says about giving and living abundant lives:

> Each of you should give what you have decided in your heart to give, not reluctantly or under compulsion, for God loves a cheerful giver. And God is able to bless you abundantly, so that in all things at all times, having all that you need, you will abound in every good work.
>
> —2 Corinthians 9:7–8.

Living a half-full life isn't just about our financial resources. It's about our entire lives, each and every aspect of them.

"No reserves, no retreats, no regrets" are handwritten words found in the Bible of William Borden, an heir to the Borden Dairy fortune, who after graduating from Yale University, rather than live a life of luxury and comfort, sailed to Egypt with the goal of reaching China to share the love of Jesus. While there, he contracted spinal meningitis and died a young man in 1913 at the age of twenty-five, but his life and death inspired countless others to volunteer for acts of service.

This idea of "glass half-full" living and the philosophy of "no reserves, no retreats, no regrets" are leading us to the same place. In sports lingo, it is the charge head coaches use all the time to "leave it all on the field." Make sense? Of course. Easy to follow? Maybe in the moment or for the big game, but what about over an entire lifetime?

Recently, a friend of mine, Katie, and a small group of friends fresh out of college who I have the honor of knowing didn't hit the job market in the traditional sense. Instead, they packed up and moved to faraway countries, putting themselves in harm's way to serve and love on people who are desperate for a better life. Places where women are second-class citizens, persecuted and discarded, places where children are sacrificed—yes, sacrificed, meaning killed in some sick ceremony—places that are just plain dark and full of evil.

If John 15:13 reads, "Greater love has no one than this, than to lay down one's life for his friends," then consider how much love does it take to risk our lives for those whom we have never met? How much love does it take to go and love on people who think we are their enemies? Seems like Katie and her friends are leaving it all on the field and not just for sixty minutes.

There is an expression that we seem to hear a lot these days: "Never let a good crisis go to waste." In politics, regardless of which side of the aisle one sits on, this is usually about spin and distraction, getting more votes, more power.

But I think the politicians have it backward. In my mind, not wasting a crisis is about giving, not getting. You see, when a crisis hits, many people get scared. They hunker in, pull back, even lose their empathy for others, which I certainly understand.

But it is in these moments of crisis when trouble hits that we need more than ever to run with abandon right into the trials and love our neighbors when their world is falling apart. We need to avoid the temptation to retreat, to run and hide, to think about ourselves first. We have to play through the pain and exhaustion, leave it all on the field, and make serving others more important than hiding out, lowering our handicap, or getting more miles on the bike. And in order to do this well, with endurance and joy, we must see the glass as half-full.

Never waste a crisis. OK then, when COVID-19 hits, let's follow our church's mission statement, "Love, love, love," and do it even more, even better. "Love, love, love" means giving goody baskets to teachers, nurses, first responders, and their families and making them personal, even down to their favorite cereal and snacks for their pets. It means getting on the phone early to pray for the elderly, to check up on the widow who is stuck alone in their house, and then taking a call late at night from someone who is depressed and just needs a friend. Love, love, love means waiting in line to get groceries in masks and delivering them to people who are at risk and can't get out. It means praying for those who are sick with COVID-19 and those who are sick from everything else. It means feeding the homeless, not running from them, and paying the rent or the mortgage for those who have nowhere to turn. Love, love, love means working with local community leaders to help provide supervision and a place for kids to do school remotely when they don't have internet access at home.

It means sacrifice for the sake of others, especially when the going gets tough. Sure, seems like this is the right way to not waste a crisis.

Half-full or half-empty? No reserve, no retreats, no regrets? Leave it all on the field, all the time? I know my vote.

Chapter 12

Timmy Time

God chose the weak things of the world to shame the strong.
—1 Corinthians 1:27

In the ancient years before the cloud, Dropbox, Google Drive, and Evernote, I kept up with important things the old-fashioned way: in files labeled by subject matter. I tend to oversave and had files bursting with information on just about every topic. Recently, as I went through the files, deciding which ones I wanted to digitize and scan, keep as is, or toss, I came across a story that had touched my heart years ago.

It is a story about a father of a child with special needs. His son was twelve years old, an age when most boys' competitive nature leaps to a new level. Testosterone is either in full force or just around the corner, and any sweetness about "playing for fun" gives way to the ambitious pursuit of victory.

The story begins when his son walks up to a group of guys playing a game of pickup baseball and asks to play. The father, hanging back a bit to give his son some freedom, is surprised when they say "yes" and then full of dread at the thought of his son actually having to make a play. He debates intervening by either making an excuse and pulling his son out or whispering to the other boys that his son is different, that he really shouldn't be out there in a competitive game.

He ends up holding back, lets his son join the others, and sits quietly on the makeshift bleachers praying that his son won't get hurt, that the other guys will treat him well and not make fun of him, and that the ball never gets hit his way—all the while wondering why God made his son the way He did. The storyteller does not ask this question in a manner that is challenging toward God, but rather in a reflective manner, one that has him thinking about the meaning of life as well as a father's concern for his son.

His prayers seem to be answered when no balls make their way to his son in the field but are seemingly unanswered when in the last inning it is his son's turn to bat. He silently cries out to God, reminding Him that while he may not have prayed specifically that he did not want his son to bat, God is God and surely knew what he meant.

"Somehow," the man's son hits the ball softly back to the pitcher, an easy out for sure. But rather than throwing the ball to first base, the pitcher looks at the batter, understanding for just a moment that there are more important things than winning. He watches as the catcher, who also gets it at this point, steers the batter, who really has no idea what to do, toward first base and helps him start running.

The pitcher throws the ball way over the first baseman's head into right field. Now everyone is onto the plan, and while the first baseman turns the man's son toward second base, the right fielder throws the ball way over the cut-off man and into left field. Ultimately, with a little help, the boy with special needs, who by almost every measure shouldn't be on the field, crosses home plate and is mobbed in celebration by players on both teams.

With tears running down his face, the father reflects partly to himself and partly to God that he now understands why his son was made the way that he is: his son is able to soften the hearts and change the behavior of others in a way that a "normal" twelve-year-old boy could never do.

This idea mentioned in 1 Corinthians 12:1—"Now about the gifts of the Spirit, brothers and sisters, I do not want you to be uninformed"—that God made us differently on purpose and does not want to remove our afflictions but rather use them is often tough to understand, accept, or celebrate in the moment. As we think about our loved ones and ourselves, we tend to long for conformity instead of accepting the fact that we are fashioned to be different, unique, and used as part of a bigger story, with each and every life celebrated and valued.

While the above-mentioned story tugs at my heart as most good stories do, it's not personal to me. I don't know the father or the son and in this era of fake news, I confess I did not even fact-check it to determine if it is a true or just a powerful work of fiction. To be honest, it does not matter much to me whether it is real or not, as I know the story in various forms is repeated all the time.

* * *

I have had the privilege of hearing Nick Vujicic speak several times. If you have never seen him or do not know his story, make sure you do and check out his video "Life Without Limbs," which you can find on YouTube, his website, and numerous other places. You see, Nick was born without any arms and or legs, and just like the boy in the previous story, Nick influences the world in ways that none of us "normal" folks can.

I have heard Nick's story about how he found hope and love in Jesus and know that he's shared this hope with people all over the globe, even in places that are hostile to those with different views and perspectives. Except in his case, Nick and his affliction, if you can even call it that, opens doors and removes boundaries—how can anyone say "no" to a guy without any arms or legs?

I have listened to Nick use his wit and wicked sense of humor to draw people to him and remind teenage girls that they are beautiful just the way they are, with no need to buy into all the things society creates to make them somehow "better" or more appealing. I've seen Nick stare down teenage boys, telling them that they are "the man" regardless of social status or the size of their biceps. There is no self-pity in Nick's talks. He lets everyone know that his condition is not a mistake, and he is just fine, thank you, with the way he is, so much so that I still remember when he told the audience with a smile that "I bet you never thought you would be jealous of someone with no arms or legs."

Nick is married, has a couple of children, and travels all around the world sharing his story and encouraging everyone he meets along the way to get going, reminding them that regardless of their circumstances, they can live a full and purposeful life. And he does all this without any arms or legs; and I grumble about my muscles being stiff, a lousy day at work, or because my refrigerator broke.

If the "boy's baseball story" got me thinking about this theme of how our afflictions are used and my time listening to Nick Vujicic made it more real, then spending time with Timothy Kriedman made it *personal.*

I remember the first time I met Timmy. I was new to Calvary Chapel Santa Barbara (CCSB for short), running late for church, and found a spot to park my car fairly close to the warehouse that serves as our sanctuary. Getting out of the car with my wife, three kids, and two cousins, I saw this man in a uniform, all of five feet tall, with a badge and all kinds of things fastened to his makeshift belt, walking intentionally and authoritatively toward us with his right hand outstretched and his index finger making a half-circular motion, summoning me like a parent might do when a child is in trouble.

I looked over my shoulder hoping to find another culprit, kind of like when you are driving and see a police officer's lights flash behind you, hoping they are for someone else, and then heave a sigh of relief when the police car drives past you in pursuit of his or her target. But in this case no one was behind me, and I found myself wondering in the ten to fifteen seconds it took him to reach me, *What have I done? And what kind of church is this?*

"Is this your first time here?" he asked. A bit confused and a little nervous, but not wanting to lie at church, even in the parking lot, I answered, "No, we have been here a few times." "OK," he said, "that spot is for first-timers, but I will let it go this time. Just don't park there again."

Years later, I still remember watching a guy who was new to our church frantically walking around our patio after service, asking everyone who this Officer Tim Kriedman was because he had signed and placed a ticket on his car telling him he would be towed if he parked in that spot again. We all just laughed.

Born with serious physical and mental limitations, Timmy was larger than life and a mainstay at CCSB long before my family and I arrived. He awoke early Sunday mornings and got a ride to church to help set up and police the parking lot with great zeal and intensity. He reminded everyone to change the batteries on their smoke detectors and in what became one of the most cherished traditions at CCSB called every single person in our church directory on a Saturday in March or April to remind us all that it was daylight savings time and to move our clocks forward and not be late for church. The move to daylight savings each spring will now forever be known fondly as "Timmy Time."

Timmy went to Heaven on March 9, 2018, just nine days short of his forty-sixth birthday. I knew Timmy in a way that many of us at CCSB did, receiving his signature greeting of "Hey, uncle" or "Hey, daddy," as all of us men were Timmy's uncle or daddy, even those quite a bit younger than him. But it was at his memorial service celebrating his life on March 18 (his birthday) that I got a glimpse of just how many people he impacted. The entire service was full of laughter and tears, the way it should be.

Pastor Tommy talked about how he is lost on Sundays now that he doesn't have Timmy there to organize things and make sure he has a glass of water on the pulpit. Some of his caregivers talked about Timmy's emotions during his never-ending series of doctor visits—nervous, grateful, and in charge but, regardless of his mood, always telling people to get to church.

Timmy volunteered at the hospital, and Pastor Doug told the story about Timmy having a pair of handcuffs attached to his belt. His supervisor decided that it was probably best that Timmy left those at home, as he had images of a patient breaking some obscure and minor rule only to end up handcuffed to a wheelchair.

Hearing from Timmy's big sister was probably the most emotional part of the service for me. She wasn't his biological sister but rather had volunteered at the place in Oregon where Timmy lived when he was a kid. Timmy never knew his real parents, and this place was a place for severely handicapped kids who often went home on the weekends and holidays. It wasn't the right place for Timmy, but since he had no family, it was where he ended up. His "sister," heartbroken, decided to bring him home with her, first occasionally and then on a regular basis; and over time, along with her sister and her dad, they became Timmy's family . . . so much so that their friends always figured that he truly was her little brother.

She shared that her greatest fear when he left Oregon years ago and moved to Devereux, a place that helps adults with various disabilities, just outside Santa Barbara, was that he would be alone. Flying down to be with him in the days before he passed away, she was shocked and overjoyed to find the hospital waiting rooms were not only not empty but overfilled with Timmy's new family, his church, so much so that people had to stand outside, praying over him and celebrating all he meant to us.

Hospital staff and doctors said they had never seen anything like it. Some asked about our church and committed to coming to see what all this love is about. Even in the ICU, during his last days when he couldn't walk or speak, our sweet Timmy was having an impact.

Stephen Hawking passed away on March 14, just five days after Timmy Kriedman. Both men had serious physical limitations, while only Timmy had serious mental limitations as well. Stephen Hawking was quite famous and a genius, a genius who spent his life trying to figure out many things: important, deep, meaningful things, which is good and beautiful.

Timmy Kriedman was not famous and definitely not a genius. Yet he figured out how to live a life that truly mattered, a life that blessed all those who knew him. And I often chuckle at the thought of him being in Heaven with a new body and a new mind, telling Billy Graham, Mother Teresa, and countless others exactly what to do . . . and where to park.

Chapter 13

Money, Money, Money

For we brought nothing into the world,
and we can take nothing out of it.
—1 Timothy 6:7

* * *

The song "For the Love of Money," released in 1973 and sung by The O'Jays, starts with them singing the word "money" five times, and since I cannot sing nor write the inflections of their voices, you will have to play the song yourself or think back to this classic and always relevant tune. It was written by Kenneth Gamble, Leon Huff, and Anthony Jackson and lists a number of inappropriate and awful things people will do for their love of money.

Unbeknownst to many, the song is actually based upon 1 Timothy 6:10, which reads, "For the love of money is a root of all kinds of evil. Some people, eager for money, have wandered from the faith and pierced themselves with many griefs."

It is important to note that the Bible does not say "*money* is a root of all kinds of evil" but rather that "the *love of money* is a root of all kinds of evil." There are plenty of wealthy people throughout history and alive today who have used and are using their financial resources in a way that honors God and gives hope to a desperate and broken world.

Looking back on my life before I focused on Jesus, I am embarrassed to point out that I talked about money more than any other topic: my family's financial status growing up, my family losing all their money, my need to make money during college, my frustration with the fact that many of my peers had wealthy parents, my decision to get rich out of college, and my bitterness that my father needed my help financially—money, money, money.

I remember with great clarity the first time I really heard Jesus's heart in regard to money. I was traveling with a friend, Ryan, in Africa, and in the midst of a long car ride, we bounced from one subject to the next before settling on the topic of stewardship. At some point in the conversation, I asked, "Do you think the 10 percent we are supposed to give is 10 percent pretax or 10 percent posttax?"

And I still remember him turning to me and saying in a soft way, "Drew, that question means you have it all you have it all wrong. You are thinking about this backward. You are asking how much of your money you want to share with God. You should be thinking about how much of God's money you want to keep from Him. You see, it all belongs to Him, and the sooner you understand this, the sooner you will receive the blessings that come from being radically generous."

Wow, talk about a wake-up call! But, if we really think about it, how much better off would the world be if I lived with this basic principle? How much better off would the world be if we all lived this way? Hmm—*it all belongs to God.* Hmm—*it's all meant to help others.*

* * *

Before passing away, my mom lived in a skilled nursing home with a strange form of dementia. Late in her life, she knew who we were, but for the most part, could not speak, was wheelchair bound, and lived in her own world without much interest in what we were doing.

She loved bananas—really loved bananas. There were always three by her bed, and this was a new thing. I don't remember her ever being a banana lover. Go figure.

Because she could not talk, she pointed to pictures on a chart when she wanted something and tried to write out requests, but her penmanship was also fading, so it was tough for us to read. She was still feisty up until the end, always was, and one time even "escaped" the facility, crossed the walkway, took an elevator up a floor, and made her way toward the pool and snack area, probably in search of more bananas. Ultimately, they had to put an alarm and seatbelt on her wheelchair. You have to laugh to keep from crying.

I do not share this story to provoke sympathy. Yes, it's sad, but she was in a great facility as far as these types of facilities go and was well taken care of for sure. Vicki thinks God kept her here on earth for a season to help make me a better son. I think she is right.

I share this story to make a broader point. As mentioned earlier, and something that should be obvious to us all, we can't take anything with us when we die. This is why time spent trying to accumulate more stuff is truly wasted time.

In the five years before passing away, my mom went from a nice two-bedroom condominium with her belongings to a one-bedroom apartment in a senior living community, still keeping her bed, her clothes, and a cell phone. Then she moved to a small room in an as-sisted living facility, where she traded in her bed for a facility-owned twin bed with bars to prevent her from falling but where she did get to keep her couch, a few tables, and some knickknacks and had a window overlooking a rose garden. And finally, she moved into a skilled nursing facility in which her only possessions were pictures, makeup (she loved her makeup), Nivea crème, and some clothes that had tags with her name stitched on them. (Not exactly a stylish look, and my mom sure did love to dress well. Talbots was her home away from home.)

I still remember when we told her about her latest and realistically last move to the skilled nursing facility. She was more coherent then and wrote down in shaky, barely legible writing, "Would I see the roses in the next room?" I keep that note in my office, which brings me to tears when I look at it or reflect on its significance. All the stuff I have, all the stuff she used to have, and now all she wanted was to be able to see a rosebush.

Vicki and I now have a new list. This list keeps track of how much money we share with God, how much we give to others. Each year, we set a goal for charitable giving, and it is pretty cool to see that number grow and its impact multiply. We are still a work in progress and can do much better, but I feel like we are heading in the right direction.

The thing about giving is that Jesus is interested in our motives. He talks about money as much as any other topic in the Bible because he knows that "for where your treasure is, there your heart will be also." (Matt. 6:21)

The world's economy looks at giving on an absolute basis: give $10,000 and get your name mentioned at the gala. Give $10,000,000 and get a wing in the library or hospital named after you. Give $100,000,000 and get your name on a business school. Give $50 and no one pays attention.

But in Jesus's economy, he looks at giving from the perspective of sacrifice. Just look at what he says in Mark 12:41–44: "Jesus sat down opposite the place where the offerings were put and watched the crowd putting their money into the temple treasury. Many rich people threw in large amounts. But a poor widow came and put in two very small copper coins worth only a few cents. Calling his disciples to him, Jesus said, 'Truly I tell you this poor widow has put more into the treasury than all the others. They all gave out of their wealth; but she, out of her poverty, put in everything—all she had to live on.'"

Talk about a foreign concept. In Jesus's economy, it is the giver of $50 who is often celebrated.

* * *

My friend Saba was raised in the midst of extreme poverty and strife between Ethiopia and Eritrea, a small country bordering Ethiopia to the north. Ever since she was little, she would get up in the middle of the night with an empty jug on her back and sneak through the bush, walking for miles to a watering hole, all the while avoiding the soldiers who tended to prey on helpless girls. Sometimes, she would find water, fill her jug, and carry it back home for her and her family to drink; other times, there would be no water, and she would make the trek back to her village empty-handed.

Saba's journey from the war and suffering in her homeland to first Saudi Arabia, then Europe, then across the ocean to San Francisco and ultimately to Santa Barbara is nothing short of a miracle. Saba makes a modest (I mean a very modest) living, and after paying her bills, she typically sends all her excess cash to Ethiopia to help her family and friends back home, who are desperately poor.

One day a couple of years ago, Saba came to my office and told me that many of her American friends were telling her that she was crazy to do this and that she needed to start thinking of herself and begin saving for her future. I love Saba's heart, but as a practical American myself, I didn't disagree that her saving just a little bit of money was an OK thing to do. She explained that if she were to put the money into her own savings account, she wouldn't be able to help herself. She'd simply take it back and give it away. So, she asked me if I would hold it for her and, no matter what, not let her take it back under any circumstances.

I was honored by her trust and confidence, agreed to help, and together, we created a ledger to keep track of the money. Then every week we would meet, and she would give me $100 to save on her behalf. This lasted about six weeks.

One day, Saba called me in tears, explaining to me that the school for blind children in Ethiopia had a problem and needed the money.

Being placed in the position by her to say "no," I reminded her that there will always be a need and she should stick to the plan. I even offered to send the money myself. But she was adamant. She said, "Drew, I know it is smart for me to save money, but I just can't do it. These people need it more than me. I will be fine, and I know I need to use this money to help these poor kids."

So, I caved, and rather quickly. I just couldn't stand in the way of Saba acting selflessly. It was in many ways, actually in most ways, a beautiful thing.

Saba comes to Vicki and me often for advice. She looks to us as mentors and advisors and in some ways, we do help her navigate life in the fast-paced Western world. But in other ways, she helps us so much more. Her sacrificial giving, determination to overcome insurmountable odds, thinking of others first, and living a life that finds its hope in Jesus often has me wondering: Who is teaching whom?

"In my Father's house are many mansions: if it were not so, I would have told you. I go to prepare a place for you. And if I go and prepare a place for you, I will come again, and receive you unto myself; that where I am, there ye may be also." (John 14:2–3). When I read this, I think of my big house, I think of the really big houses in Montecito, Beverly Hills, or the Hamptons. I think of the wealth and opulence in the world, and I think about Saba's small apartment crammed with people from all over the world. Knowing that God's ways are not our ways, I often pray, "Lord, I hope my place in Heaven is in Saba's neighborhood—that I get to spend time in the really big house that you have most certainly prepared for her."

* * *

A couple of years ago, our church heard about the Saho people, a group of about 240,000 people living in northern Ethiopia and Eritrea. We learned that they were hoping to get a Bible translated into their native language, and we agreed to help them take the first step to fulfilling this dream by partnering with Seed Company, a leading Bible translator. We committed to raising the funds needed to translate the Gospel of Luke, thus bringing the first pages of scripture ever in the Saho language alive.

We explained to the folks in our church what we were doing and taped large sheets of paper on the walls in our foyer with all the verses found in Luke written on them. The cost to translate each verse was about $30 and we invited everyone in our church to adopt a verse or verses after service. People could come out and make a donation and put their name next to the verse or verses they wanted to support. It was pretty cool to see our church embrace this project, and some people rushed out of the service or even left a little early to sign up for their favorite verse. Some folks adopted a number of verses, one for each member of the family, and some just said, "I'll take ten or twenty verses; you pick them."

By the second weekend, most of the verses were chosen and we were in the home stretch of completing our task. But, it was after the first service on this second Sunday that my heart was touched in an unexpected way. I was standing in our breezeway collecting donations when I noticed a guy from our church pacing back and forth from one end of the hallway to another. He had a piece of paper and a pen and explained to me that he found three verses that were not yet taken, and he was going into the second service and would pray about which of the three verses God wanted him to fund.

OK, this guy was serious, and he came out right after the service and told me with great conviction and certainty, "I know the verse God wants me to adopt." Sure enough, it was the only one of the three verses that had yet to be taken, as the others had been chosen by someone else while he was praying.

At this point, he pulled his wallet out of his pocket, and the first thing I noticed was that there were no credit cards, which is atypical these days (and certainly not the norm for Santa Barbara or our church). He opened the billfold and pulled out all his cash: $12. "Oh shucks," he said.

I told him that I knew he was the right person to help translate this verse and he could just bring the rest of the money next week or that he and I could share the verse. I really did not care about getting his $18 and was just trying to get him to feel good about "owning" the verse. Clearly, he needed to play a role in this project.

After some discussion and me encouraging him to put his name on the verse, he did so, left me with the $12, and said, "I will be right back," and off he went.

I didn't think much about him or our visit after he left. I was busy collecting funds from others and visiting with people as they left the church. About fifteen minutes later, as I was reconciling things for the day, he came running back in, emptying his pockets with crumpled dollar bills and change, all kinds of change—quarters, dimes, nickels, and pennies. It was pretty clear we were getting the bulk of this guy's stash. Laying everything on the table in front of us, he had exactly $18. I reiterated that he really did not need to use what appeared to be every last dollar he had, but he replied with emotion and determination, "Thanks, but I really do need to do this. I am sure God wants me to."

This story illustrates what Jesus was saying about the poor widow. He celebrates those who give generously, those who give from the heart. Driving home that day, I was conflicted by the fact that this gentleman, Jeff, was giving far more than I was, not in absolute terms but in terms of sacrifice. This does not mean that large gifts are not good or needed. Solving the big issues in this world requires vast amounts of money. The challenge for those of us with an abundance of resources is this: Can we look at money in the same manner that the widow in the Bible and my new friend Jeff do?

I think, in some ways, it is more difficult for affluent people to share sacrificially. After all, we are used to certain comforts, and giving them up is not easy, while people who have less have never experienced those comforts and so have less to give up.

The reality is, I like stuff. Perhaps you do as well—that is the way of this world.

Truth is, whenever I share the story of our church helping translate the gospel of Luke into the Saho language, it's Jeff's story that stirs my heart the most because it's genuine, pure, and without the fanfare that often follows those of us who write the big checks.

Chapter 14

Be the Man

Life's most persistent and urgent question
is, "What are you doing for others?"
—Dr. Martin Luther King, Jr

I love action heroes; I think most guys do. Books, TV shows, and movies in which the tough good guy overcomes insurmountable odds to get the bad guys are always fun. Some of my friends and I even debate which tough guy is the toughest. Who would win in a fight? James Bond, Jason Bourne, or Jack Reacher from the best-selling books written by Lee Child? Weapons or no weapons, up close or from a distance? That kind of stuff.

In some ways, the entertainment industry gets it right. As written in the book *The Divine Conspiracy Continued* by Dallas Willard and Gary Black, Jr., "A saint or hero is one who to a significant degree chooses to forgo or to risk forgoing the enjoyment of goods or even necessities, perhaps life itself, for the sake of advancing the good of others." That sounds like James Bond to me: risking his life multiple times to save the world from evil.

But in other ways, the entertainment industry is just that—entertainment, not an accurate depiction of real life. In the movies, the hero almost always wins, gets the girl, and lives happily ever after . . . at least until the sequel. But in real life, doctors, nurses, first responders, teachers, missionaries, and countless other heroes live without fanfare, glamor, or recognition. Some even sacrifice their lives for the sake of others, choosing to live a full life, a courageous life, rather than a safe one.

So, be the man! Does that mean we are to be the baddest dude or the most macho guy avenging all wrongs or perceived slights by crushing those who get in our way, seeking revenge when necessary and never, ever backing down? No! But it also doesn't mean that we are to avoid or run from conflict and confrontation either.

God wants us to seek justice and he wants us to love people. Why is this so hard? Part of our difficulty is that we tend to confuse meekness with weakness. Meekness means "strength under control"—doing the right thing in the right way. Weakness means "lacking strength," which means we either cower and punt when the going gets tough or join the mob because it's easy.

If we truly want to help, if we truly want to lead, we must learn to stay meek, stay strong, and stay under control. If we really want to put forth lasting change, we need to take a look at how Jesus views leadership: "If anyone desires to be first, he shall be last of all and servant of all" (Mark 9:35). In other words, it isn't about what we get from this life, but what we give to this life. It isn't about being first all the time. It's about making sure others finish first.

Knowing that Jesus teaches with humility, how do we lead the same way? First, we must understand that humility is not false self-deprecation but rather finding joy when we have no power, recognition, or authority. Then, we must acknowledge that true humility is rare, especially in those with stature and power.

* * *

Hector Chacon is one of my heroes, which, knowing Hector, would embarrass him greatly. Hector grew up on the streets of Honduras, orphaned and homeless, doing whatever he had to survive as a teenager in those circumstances. One day, God intervened in the form of an offer by President Ronald Reagan—not that the president actually wrote Hector, but the US government posted a letter signed by President Reagan inviting a limited number of students from developing countries, including Honduras, to apply for grants to attend certain colleges in the US to learn skills they could then use to help the economic conditions back in their home countries.

Hector applied, was accepted, attended the University of Texas at El Paso, and ultimately graduated with a degree in engineering. Then, he did something that few students who get a taste of life in America do—he returned home to Honduras to help his country with his newfound skills.

Today, Hector is head of Water Mission's efforts in Honduras and a member of the Water Mission board. With Hector at the helm, Water Mission has become one of the largest employers in the Colón region of Honduras. To date, they've completed hundreds of projects across the country, led a major sanitation and health impact study in the region, and are now completing projects in neighboring countries such as El Salvador and Guatemala. But, while Hector's resume is impressive, it is the intangibles that make him truly special.

Having traveled to work with Hector and Water Mission with numerous youth groups over the years, I can tell you that Hector is the boss, no question about it, and he certainly has authority over his staff. But you wouldn't know it from the way he interacts with them. He is perfectly content standing in the background, humbly giving others the credit and empowering those around him to do their best. These traits, along with a wicked sense of humor, make him what business books would call a "level five leader."

"Fifteen minutes" is Hector's standard response to the ongoing question from the kids about how long it will take to get from one village to another. Letting you in on a little secret: There is nothing just fifteen minutes away in Honduras. An inadequate highway infrastructure, bumpy and winding roads, and police checkpoints (among other things) all make sure of that.

Over the years, we've grown close with Hector, and during one of our trips, I was able to spend some time with him while visiting a plot of land he bought to, hopefully, build a medical center for people in the surrounding villages. Many of the people in the remote parts of Honduras only have access to healthcare via missionaries and humanitarian groups that come for a short while and then leave. The care provided by these groups is well intentioned and helpful, but also sporadic and without the facilities needed to provide adequate long-term care.

I have stood with him on the hill at the top of his property overlooking the valley below and listened to him share his dream for his people, give thanks to God for the life he has been given, and pray for all those Hondurans who are struggling and suffering. Hector's heart is pure; Hector's heart is about others.

Because our trips are packed to the brim, our time together is like being part of one big extended family, if only for a week or so, and I love the fact we get to spend time with Hector as well as his wife and kids. I think one of the big life lessons from these trips is the way the young people we bring from back home get a chance to see Hector—the big cheese—love on his team and family in the midst of hard work and great purpose. It is no surprise that Hector regularly tops the list of the most impactful people we meet on these trips. I know he tops my list.

* * *

Vicki and I first met Tommy and Debi Schneider for a cup of coffee in the mountains of Colorado. We had mutual friends who said we just had to meet, and because they lived in the Vail Valley and we spent a bunch of time up there, we got together in a kind of couples' blind date.

Well, we hit it off, and as we became good friends, then the best of friends, I soon learned that Pastor Tommy (or PT for short) and Deb were kind of famous in this part of the world, and not just because he was in *People* magazine for renewing the vows of the original Bachelor and his wife.

Trips to the supermarket or out to dinner were always accompanied by hugs from all the people they loved and impacted. Seriously, I have never seen anything like it. I could hang out there for a month and not visit with anyone other than my family, but try to go get a cup of coffee with PT, and the next thing you know, there is laughter, tears, hugs, and prayer all over the place.

The thing is that both Tommy and Deb are intentional about loving people. While I am sure that is part of the job of a pastor and his wife, I feel like they take it to a whole other level. Get on a chairlift with other skiers or snowboarders who you don't know and there is often silence or a few minutes of awkward conversation. Not with Tommy, who by the time we get off the lift knows everybody's names, has them laughing or crying or both with one of his stories, and has asked how he can pray for them.

Sent out to start a church twenty-plus years ago, this special couple has helped transform a ski town by meeting people from all walks of life, from all over the world, and loving them unconditionally. And now they are doing the same thing in Santa Barbara, as a few years ago, they followed their hearts to head west, exchanging the mountains for the beaches, where they continue to love people and lead our church.

Love means seeking, caring, and helping even when we don't feel like it. Love means helping people we don't even like. "What the World Needs Now Is Love'" was written by Burt Bacharach and Hal David and sung by many. The lyrics are lived by Tommy and Debi Schneider big-time. May we all follow their lead and do the same.

* * *

When Brent Reichard and his brother Bruce were teenagers, they tragically lost their father in a plane crash. Their family was split, and the crash really did a number on their stepmom, who survived but was really never the same. With their real mom remarried, their father gone, and their stepmom dealing with her own trauma, they were pretty much on their own.

Dealing with the unthinkable, this is one of those moments where the saying "What doesn't kill you makes you stronger" actually fits perfectly. Getting up off the ground, Brent went to work at a local hamburger stand to make a few bucks, worked hard, learned the ropes, and eventually bought the place. Fast-forward, and the Reichard brothers are restaurant icons. The Habit Burger Grill is now all over the world, providing great food to an increasing number of loyal fans.

But the real story isn't about their work ethic or success. Their legacy is about how they lead, how they serve, how they give back. In Santa Barbara where it all started, they're part of the fabric of the community—serving in one of their mobile Habit trucks whenever a good cause needs some help and giving through their free burger coupons, which tend to show up at just about every event.

Brent's business card reads "Chief Burger Flipper." No fancy titles here, and when you walk into one of their restaurants, you'll find a story on a plaque about how it all got started, which is inspiring and draws people in.

One night at LAX while Brent and I were traveling together, we ventured into a Habit for a late dinner before hopping on our flight to Santa Barbara.

Of course, none of the workers knew the founder was standing right in front of them, and Brent surely wasn't going to say anything. The "Do you know who I am?" nonsense is not part of his vocabulary. He simply walks up and places an order: "A Charburger and fries, please." Of course, I couldn't resist, and told everyone who he was. Pretty soon, all the workers were taking pictures with the humble founder who dusted off his boots in the most difficult of circumstances and built something wonderful, something to last, and did it his way, the right way.

In the words of Frank Sinatra, "I did it my way." In the case of Brent Reichard, thank goodness.

* * *

My old boss, Bob Donato, recently went to Heaven after a lengthy battle with ALS, or Lou Gehrig's disease as it is often called. It is an awful disease, and without getting into the graphic details, let's just say if you are feeling sorry for yourself, remember that compared with those with ALS, there are no bad days. Yet, Bob and his wife Vivian tackled his condition with the same zeal, determination, and positivity with which they have tackled the rest of their lives.

They simply would not let his condition define them. Instead, they set out to help raise money to fund research with a hope to find a cure for this dreaded disease. They continued to live to the fullest as much as they could, never seeking sympathy but rather seeking to help and comfort others. All this got me thinking. *How does one stay so positive in the midst of such a gnarly trial?* As one of the speakers at Bob's memorial service said, Bob had faith. He trusted God and accepted his condition as part of a bigger plan. He made the choice to live and live fully, even when he was sick.

During this season of his life, being a selfless man, Bob came to my son's wedding ceremony despite the difficulty of traveling. Bob knew me in my early adult days before kids and knew Spencer his entire life. What started out as a business relationship had become so much more. As Bob often said, "We now focus on the important stuff."

After the wedding and among the crowd, we sought each other out. Bob is a tough guy, one of the toughest, but he also is an emotional man. With tears running down his face, he let go of his walker and just wrapped his arms around me. Holding each other, I know God gave me these words to share with him, important words: "Bob, you are the greatest of men. Days like this do not happen unless men like you pour into men like me. From the bottom of my heart, thank you." With us now crying together, time stood still for a minute. I had a once-in-a-lifetime moment that I will never forget with a man I will never forget.

And this is why we all must get to a point where we have the maturity to share our wisdom with others whom we are close to, like Bob did for me. We cannot spend our entire lives just accepting wisdom from others, although that is a lifetime pursuit. We must also pay our blessings forward, be a mentor to those around us, share wisdom that comes from experience, and lift up others to become better people, better leaders.

Thank you, Bob, for all you did for me and my family and so many others. You are simply the best.

* * *

While Hector Chacon, Tommy and Debi Schneider, Brent Reichard, and Bob Donato fall in the category of unsung heroes like most heroes in the real world do, Seth Godin has a platform. He's a successful entrepreneur, best-selling author, sought-after public speaker, and an advisor and friend to long a list of who's who across a variety of industries and disciplines.

I have had the privilege of knowing Seth for the last twenty years or so, and here is the thing: Seth doesn't act like he is a big shot. He says "please" and "thank you," is considerate, shows up on time, and does what he says he will do.

Time with Seth is likely to push the boundaries and explore possibilities with intellectual curiosity. From trying the most famous "dive" taco joints around Los Angeles to sampling his favorite chocolate bars gathered from his many trips around the world to the more serious stuff, Seth asks the right questions and pushes those around him to do better, to be better. As a one-of-a-kind thinker and communicator, Seth has spent a good portion of his life teaching and coaching others. He uses his gifts and influence to lift up and bring attention to those doing good things as well as help those who are hurting or marginalized.

From launching one of the world's most popular blogs and faithfully posting it each and every day, to his twenty best-selling books, to his

Akimbo workshops that have helped thousands of people learn to make better decisions and lead well, Seth, like my old boss, Bob, is paying it forward big time, and the world is a better place because of him.

Not all of us will move the needle the way Seth does. But we can all find those folks like him to lean into, those folks who inspire us to do more, to grow and be better. And we certainly can do what Seth does by sharing and caring, even away from the limelight in personal ways, ways that go unnoticed. Sometimes it's the little stuff, the stuff we do when no one is looking, that is most important and shows who we really are.

* * *

Peter Trabucco is one of my closest friends. He and I end every conversation or text with "I love you." Our kids grew up together and still hang out, and I imagine they will be lifelong friends as well.

For over twenty-five years, Peter taught second grade at a small Christian school in Santa Barbara. When asked why second grade, he always answers the same way: "Because in second grade, I can still make it up if I don't know the answer." Of course, he is kidding, and he also tells the kids, usually on the first day of class, that he used to be six feet tall, which confuses them quite a bit because Peter is a functioning quadriplegic and in a wheelchair. He has limited use of his hands and obviously cannot walk, but fortunately he can breathe on his own.

I met Peter years after "the accident," which came when he jumped off some rocks onto what turned out to be a shallow shelf in a river. But rather let this event and the aftermath define him, Peter got married, had two wonderful twin girls (who, thanks to the marvels of modern healthcare, are his biological kids), and set forth with a life of purpose and service.

I still remember my son at the end of his time in Peter's class, sitting at his desk crying because he just couldn't imagine a school day without Mr. Trabucco, an image that has been repeated on the last day of school countless times over the years.

In addition to being a top-rate teacher, Peter has that intangible ability to lead and to inspire. He's popular and effective in part because he is a guy (and at the risk of offending some, let's be honest—most second grade teachers are women, at least in my town), in part because he's in a wheelchair and blind in one eye (which makes him unique and relatable to kids who are intrigued by the whole thing), and in part because he never, ever lives like his condition is a burden.

Peter drives his own car, refuses to use handicap spots, travels, and pretty much lives life like the rest of us. He is not a guy in a wheelchair but rather a really cool dude who just happens to be in a wheelchair. Big difference.

Love you, Peter Trabucco!

* * *

The live auction at most fundraisers typically includes exotic vacations and extravagant items and experiences. It is when the big bucks are raised. I am too picky of a traveler to bid on trips and golf with so and so, and backstage passes to the hottest new group or artist might appeal to others, but not to me. I am not starstruck and at times go the other way, avoiding that scene altogether. But when I heard that we could donate funds to UC Santa Barbara's athletic department for an evening with John Wooden, I was in. This was, for me, one of those "price is no object" moments.

John Wooden led UCLA basketball teams to ten national titles in twelve seasons, including seven straight titles. His teams won a record eighty-eight games without a loss and went undefeated for an entire season a record four times.

The "wizard of Westwood," as he was often called, was arguably the most successful coach of all time. OK, I know times have changed. College hoops is now "one and done," when in Coach Wooden's era, freshmen could not even play varsity basketball. How would he have fared in today's NCAA? Legitimate question.

But while we can certainly debate what his win–loss record would be today or the number of titles he would win with a sixty-four-team field during March Madness, we all must concede that his impact on his players and all those who knew him was profound and everlasting.

Needless to say, at the auction, I took home the prize, and a few friends and I got to spend an evening with the legendary coach. After dinner and a sweet time of conversation, we headed to his house for a bit. We peppered him with questions about his famous sayings, "No whining, no complaining, no excuses" and "Never lie, never cheat, never steal," phrases that he attributed to his father. Dads, are you listening?

We went through his Pyramid of Success, which provides all of us a road map for individual and team excellence, the same road map he used to build a legacy unmatched in the game of basketball. He explained that the pyramid offered no explicit reference to basketball or athletics and that his diagram is simply a road map to becoming a better person. This is why his rules included "Never score without acknowledging a teammate," "One word of profanity, and you're done for the day," and "Treat your opponent with respect." Wouldn't it be great if today's top coaches and athletes led like Coach Wooden?

We even got him to share about how he started the season teaching the players how to put on their socks so they would not get blisters. We laughed at his famous story about how the team's best player, Bill Walton, showed up to practice with a full beard, which was against the rules, insisting it was his right to grow his hair and beard any way he wanted. Coach Wooden explained how he asked Bill if he believed that strongly in his beard, and when Walton said he did, Coach replied, "That's good. I admire people who have strong beliefs and stick by them, I really do. We're going to miss you." End of story, as the All-American center was quickly clean-shaven.

Turns out, Bill Walton and John Wooden remained close friends long after college, and the night we sat in Coach Wooden's home, Bill

Walton called several times. Each time, Coach Wooden would pick up the phone, talk to Bill for a brief moment, and then explain he had guests and say goodnight. It was actually really sweet to witness their affection for each other and the way that Bill Walton revered John Wooden.

This was one of the things from that evening that stood out to me and that I think is rare in successful people. John Wooden was a man of great stature. I mean, come on, the UCLA court is named after him and his wife. Most of us will never obtain his stature in our lifetime. Yet, he never made us feel that way. He never made us feel rushed, like we were a burden or that we had a finite amount of time with him based on the terms of some agreement. When we finally left a little before midnight for the long drive back home, we all felt like he would have allowed us to stay longer if we wished.

As much as we wanted to talk about basketball and all those great players and championships (and we certainly got our fill of those topics), Coach Wooden wanted to talk about his faith, his wife, and his family. He shared with us how after his wife died on March 21, 1985, he wrote a letter to her on the twenty-first of each month, a tradition that carried on until he passed away in 2010 at the age of ninety-nine. His relationship with God, unconditional love for his wife, and commitment to family, not NCAA championships or fame, were most important to him. Let us all learn from his example.

Coach Wooden graciously wrote a personal note to me and each of my kids in his book and on his Pyramid of Success, which are now all framed to avoid wear and tear. These remain among my most cherished gifts and have been a constant source of wisdom over the years.

As John Wooden once said, "Success is peace of mind which is a direct result of self-satisfaction in knowing you did your best to become the best you are capable of becoming." These are words to live by.

* * *

At some point in my adult life, I latched onto the statement "My life in the future will be the same except for the people I meet, the places I go, and the experiences I have."

With that in mind lies the answer to the following question: "What do Hector Chacon, Tommy and Deb Schneider, Brent Reichard, Bob Donato, Seth Godin, Peter Trabucco, and John Wooden have in common?" Not a darn thing, except for the big, important things like service, excellence, integrity, and perseverance.

If we really want to be "the man" and live a life full of joy, purpose, and adventure, then we have to keep moving and striving. We must turn our thinking upside down and instead of asking "What do I want from life?," ask "What does life want from me? What does this world need from me?" If we all did this, imagine the possibilities.

Chapter 15

The Good, the Bad, the Ugly

*The three most important ways to lead people are
. . . by example . . . by example . . . by example.*
—Albert Schweitzer

Harry Chapin's "Cat's in the Cradle" may be one of the more depressing songs about a father who never found time for his son, only to grow old and realize that now his son cannot find any time for him, but it does make a point that how we raise our kids has a lifetime of consequences.

If you've ever entered a raffle contest, you have probably heard the words or read the disclaimer, "Do not need to be present to win." The fine print for being a good parent actually reads the opposite: "Must be present to win." We can't expect a relationship with our kids if we are gone all the time, hanging out with our friends, or checked out even when we are in the same house or room.

There have been a couple of times over my career in which I have been encouraged to move to New York City and become part of "corporate." In each case, the "pitch" was greater status, a bigger title, and more cash. In each case, my decision to say "no" was easy for two reasons: one, we are all a product of our upbringing to some extent, and I just could not shake the images of my father's struggles after he was forced to stop climbing the corporate ladder; and two, I did not want to miss out on my kids growing up, which tends to happen when you're advancing in management at a large corporation. All along, I wanted to make a nice living, spend time with my family, and be the soccer coach.

My story is my story, and none of this is meant to pass judgment on others or disparage those parents who travel a fair amount to provide for their families or climb the corporate ladder. I know a handful of moms and dads who hop on an airplane a fair amount and make it a priority to get home for the important stuff, even when it means catching a red-eye or leaving on a 6 a.m. flight. For instance, my good friend, John Davies, has traveled for years running the public affairs firm he founded. Yet, he is a present father, a dad who has flown home from the East Coast on a Thursday and then back out Friday morning just to make sure he doesn't miss a game or school function. He understands what it means to be present and knows with certainty the stark reality that our kids do not want more stuff—they want more of us.

* * *

I love sports. I love playing sports, I love coaching sports, and I love watching sports, both live in-person and on TV or on my iPad. My wife constantly reminds me that the players and referees cannot hear me when I yell at the TV even though the refs are always against my team (just kidding—sort of).

There is an old saying, "If you want to see depravity, watch our political leaders or listen to parents when their kids are playing sports." This is actually my saying, but I am convinced it's true. I coached all my kids: in soccer, basketball, baseball (which was the hardest), and softball—everything but volleyball, which is the sport they all ended up playing in high school (told you God has a sense of humor). But even with volleyball, which I know little about, I couldn't help myself, dissecting every play and providing unsolicited advice on ways for them to improve after every game. Note to parents: just shut up—it isn't helpful.

Early in my coaching season of life, a parent actually complained because his daughter was playing too much. If we are honest, none of us parents ever complain because our kids are getting too much playing time, but this dad did. It was hilarious. At this level, American Youth Soccer Organization (AYSO) soccer games consist of playing four quarters rather than two halves like traditional grown-up soccer. In the third quarter, I would take our two best players out so the rest of the girls would have to learn to play without them. At the younger ages, there are always a couple of ringers who dominate the game, and I wanted all the girls to have a chance to step up. Well, my decision drove this dad crazy. He would pull me aside and say, "Drew, I just really want the win. Take my daughter out—she is not that good." *Seriously, she's nine and doing fine.*

But much more frequently, it was the opposite. When my son was ten, there was a kid on our team whose parents watched every practice and brought an entourage to every game (I mean like fifteen people), and every game, they would complain that their son wasn't getting enough touches. I would patiently tell them that it is a team sport, blah, blah, blah, blah, blah. Finally, I'd had enough. I wasn't getting paid enough to get beat up by this family every single Saturday. A gift certificate at the end of the season and a coach's trophy is a nice gesture, but let's just say I wasn't in this for the money or recognition. Fire me, please!

I finally told them that of the twelve kids on our team, their son was somewhere between the third and fifth best player, and that the two best players were significantly better. Neither of the best players was my son, so this made our talk a little easier. What I was telling them was obvious to me and everyone else, but they just couldn't see it. They thought their boy was bound for the Olympics and headed to Europe to play for Manchester United, and I, the unpaid, bungling AYSO coach, was standing in the way. I certainly didn't want to crush their dreams, and I know that kids mature at different times, and anything can happen. But those are long odds to begin with, and if you are not a dominant player at age nine, chances are you probably won't be making a living playing soccer.

I've seen parents get in fistfights on the sideline: grown men and women yelling obscenities at referees who are often high school kids making $20 a game. One year, I watched a coach "accidently" tell a couple of the less talented kids on the team the wrong time to show up for the game. He whispered to me that if we didn't have to play them, we could take the league. It took him a while to figure out that I was the one giving their parents the right time.

Why is it that our children's sports spark such emotion in us as parents? I could share endless stories proving my point about depravity being at its finest during youth sporting events, but I need to move on and actually make a point, so I'll just leave you with the following.

Today's athletes are treated like Roman gladiators back in the ancient days. More civilized, yes, but revered by the masses as if somehow insane physical talent translates to king-like status. In a culture that is prestige driven, in a way, we as parents can be validated when our kids are great athletes.

For the most part, my children have always been good but not great at sports. They have always been an important part of the team but not one of the stars of the team. (Sorry, kids, wrong gene pool.) And on the occasion when they really stood out, I enjoyed their successes and the accolades that came my way with perhaps a little too much pride creeping in.

I love sports, and competitive sports play a critical role in the development of young people. They serve as a building block for our kids to lead productive lives as adults and teach valuable lessons, including sacrifice, teamwork, and leadership. I just think at the end of the day, our youth should be celebrated more for their character than their athletic abilities. Wonder what God thinks.

* * *

Unfortunately, sports are not the only arena in which parents misbehave. Over fifty people have been charged and twenty-plus people have pleaded guilty for their roles in the 2019 college admissions scandal, in which parents made up a bunch of stuff and paid a great deal of money to get their kids into "good schools."

Seth Godin calls this out for what it is: "We often say 'good college' when we mean 'famous college.' And so, the college one goes to doesn't tell us very much at all about what someone learned, or even about who they are. It merely demonstrates that when they were 18 years old, a combination of luck and signaling led to them being chosen (or not)."

Yet, here we are as parents, hopefully not going to the lengths of the people in the scandal, but still hiring college admission coaches and essay specialists, pulling strings with influential alumni and pressuring teachers for a higher grade or class ranking, and on and on, just so we can tell everybody that Johnny got into this school or Susie will be attending this prestigious university in the fall.

This is not a rant against helping our kids achieve great things. We should be all about achievement. Nor am I suggesting that we cannot do both—achieve great things and be a great person. It is a matter of getting the order right.

The priority for our kids should be "eulogy virtues," as David Brooks calls them in his book *The Road to Character*. Eulogy virtues are those things that people talk about at our funerals, the ones that exist at the core of our being. And it is these things that we should be pushing on our kids with more energy and oversight than their "resume virtues," the things that get them into grad school or a good job. Sounds like a subtle distinction, but trust me, it isn't.

I received a text from my son's old college roommate, Riley, a while back. It was a group text sent to a handful of people who usually banter about sports, politics, or just silly guy stuff. Riley is one of those kids who is genius. As his mom says, he could have skipped three or four grades, which in one way is good, but in another makes him a bit of a handful (her words, not mine). Riley was student body president as an undergrad, graduated near the top of his class in law school, and has now moved on to big-name law firms and a sought-after clerkship. In short, he is on the fast track for a life of achievement.

But his question in our group text wasn't about any of this. It was about how to correctly share a portion of his still modest income even in the midst of paying off student loan debt. It was about his commitment to God to give back even when he doesn't have much to give. It was about his heart and his character and making sure he has his priorities in order.

I am fired up that Riley gets it and that he sought me and others out to check himself. But so many other people his age don't understand giving: they're just following the lessons learned at home. And this is why being a "prestige-driven" parent is dangerous because while we all want our kids to do well, the push to have them recognized for worldly pursuits above all else often results in us pushing the boundaries of what is right and wrong and minimizing those traits that Jesus values, like humility, a servant heart, others first, and honesty, to name a few.

These are values we should aim to instill in our children—and in ourselves. One of my long-time friends, Sol, who is a highly successful scientist and entrepreneur, ended each and every day when his kids were little with what he called "the Chucky Test," named after his son Chuck, where he would ask himself how Chucky would feel if he shared all the things he did at work. Sol's thought was pretty simple: if I can't tell my young son the truth, the whole truth, and nothing but the truth, then shame on me.

Jacqueline Novogratz is the founder and CEO of the Acumen Fund, a group that is at the forefront of thinking differently about how the world tackles poverty. In her book *Manifesto for a Moral Revolution*, she talks about the strict ethical code that all of Acumen's partners must adhere to for them to work together. She describes a real-life example of exiting an investment because the entrepreneur insisted on keeping two sets of books, saying, "That's just the way it works." Maybe, but it shouldn't be, and Jacqueline and her team let him know in no uncertain terms that the phrase "everybody does it" doesn't cut it. "It is either legal or illegal, ethical or unethical."

Sounds righteous and smart, and like a pretty darn good value system to me—much better than closing our eyes and conforming to what everybody else is doing. Sounds like principles we should teach our kids.

* * *

"Failure is not an option" is a phrase often associated with Gene Kranz and the Apollo 13 moon mission, and the tagline of the 1995 film *Apollo 13*.

Here is the thing about raising kids: "failure is an option." As hard as it is, let them fail, let them fail, let them fail. No, I am not being harsh or uncaring. We must let our children fail because it is through adversity, not prosperity, that they will grow. It is by falling down and being forced to get back up that they will develop the character and resilience to make an impact for good in this world. Not only that, "but we also glory in our sufferings, because we know that suffering produces perseverance; perseverance, character; and character, hope" (Rom. 5:3–4).

* * *

One of my favorite leadership principles is "7–10s only," which is a clever reminder to focus on the big stuff, not the little things. By rating each issue that comes my way, I can take immediate action on the 10s and avoid allowing the 1s to be a distraction. If my attention drifts into the 3s and the 4s, then I am probably not going to be effective. Funny how this is so much easier in business than in family life. But if we are going to survive and thrive as parents, we need to learn to pick our battles and not sweat the small stuff. 7–10s only, please.

* * *

Laugh-In was a hit show back in the late 1960s starring Dick Martin and Dan Rowan and featuring many of the stars of the day, including Goldie Hawn and Lily Tomlin. It was a silly show, sort of like a tamer version of *Saturday Night Live*, full of fast-paced, impromptu skits and jokes with the cohosts making fun of themselves and everyone else in a good-natured manner.

One of the best ways to keep our kids close and our families together is to follow the example set by *Laugh-In* and be creative, mix it up, and get out of the routine, all the while laughing with one another, for one another.

For years, every summer I would host "Daddy Camp" for a week, where we would stay at home and have different activities each day. Some of the most talked about Daddy Camps are those when we had Hamburger Helper for breakfast, ate spaghetti with no hands (hint: use lots of towels), and the time our son put fish bait in his sister's hair and had her wander into the shallow water, thinking it would help him catch fish. She was "all in" until she realized the fish bait didn't smell so good and his fishing line and hooks kept hitting her. Thankfully, none of the hooks caught her, and while we didn't catch any fish (big surprise), we also did not end up in the emergency room, so overall, it was a win.

One day, when my kids were teenagers, we were looking at old photos together, and my daughters commented on the fact that I used to look younger and have more hair, and that none of it was gray. So, I marched them both into the bathroom, stood next to them, and pointed to the mirror and said, "That's the reason—that's the reason I have gray hair. That's the reason I have less hair." It took a few tries for them to get my humor and realize I was pointing at them.

A short time after the "mirror episode," I was in a casual restaurant in an airport and the waiter asked me for my ID. *Ha!* I thought, and then quickly texted our family group chat, "I just got carded; guess who looks pretty darn young for his age?" The joke was on me when a couple came into the restaurant a few minutes later, one with a cane and the other with a walker and, you guessed it, the waiter asked them for their IDs. Duh, it's an airport in a post-9/11 world. Sitting close to them, I told them my story and they agreed to pose for a picture holding up their IDs, which I then sent to the same group text, much to the delight of everyone in my family. Except for me.

As parents, we set the tone for our families, and as kids grow older and schedules get more packed, the stakes get higher. It is easy for the family unit to get really serious and become more like an office—task driven—and less like a family. When teenage life intrudes, your kids will be stressed, so stop on occasion, be silly, think out of the box, and laugh as much as possible. Laughter really is the best medicine.

* * *

We had friends, Esther and Dieter, who lived in a small town in Germany adjacent to the Black Forest. I say "had" because Dieter recently passed away. They were quite a bit older than us, and we first met them after their daughter, Iris, who was part of our Bible study group at church, unexpectedly died from a heart attack at a young age. They flew in from Germany to Santa Barbara devastated, as any parent would be after losing a child. Needing a place to stay for a week or so, we put them up in our little guesthouse, and Vicki and I got a glimpse at what a marriage should look like when we saw them holding hands by candlelight each night, praying together. We watched them love each other and hold on to their faith in the midst of overwhelming tragedy.

While this experience was in response to a terrible loss, it does make the point that we need to love our spouse, support one another, and pray together—for our marriage, for our kids—in the good times and the tough times. Our children are watching us and need to know that mom and dad are solid and committed to each other and to them.

* * *

Jeopardy!, hosted for years by the late Alex Trebek, was the quintessential game show for really smart people. When watching, I'd find myself knowing the answers only in the categories where many of the actual participants struggled, namely sports and entertainment. Guess they hung with a different crowd, but as someone who likes to think I am somewhat intelligent, the whole experience is humbling, to say the least. Those folks sure know a lot of stuff.

When it comes to family life, I think I'd do a bit better than as a *Jeopardy!* Contestant and get at least a few of the answers right.

"Name three important words that, when spoken in humility, keep a family close."

"What is 'I am sorry'?"

I still remember the surprise and relief in my kids' eyes the first time I told them that I was sorry, that it was my fault. Sounds easy, sounds humble, but often these three simple words are absent among us grown-ups.

"A word that shows an inability to engage in conversation or defend your point of view, especially when there is disagreement."

"What is 'Whatever'?"

When my kids were young, I used to fine them a dollar whenever they said "whatever." OK, so I didn't always enforce the punishment, but think I did make the point that "whatever" is just plain lazy, and that the ability to discuss differing opinions in a respectful manner is great way to grow and learn, but only if we can control our emotions and articulate why we believe what we do.

Might as well teach these necessary life skills when our kids are young.

Don't raise your voice. Improve your argument. Don't walk away. Don't storm out of the room in a huff; instead, explain to me why I am wrong or say so when you are. Acknowledge you messed up, or if I did, offer me grace and a better path.

Want to keep your family close? Want to help your children learn to problem solve? Say the right words, give solid answers, and ask the right questions.

* * *

Whether it is us striving to get more of whatever we are chasing or doing our best to make sure our kids don't get a bad grade, get cut from the team, or sit in detention for doing something stupid, at the core it is all about our (us parents) own insecurity.

The world gives us a grade based on how our kids are doing; their lives are a reflection of us. So, we often protect them and shelter them from the consequences of their actions in part so no one will ever think badly of them, but mostly so no one ever will ever think badly of us.

But here is why that doesn't work. Eventually, they will leave (eventually, they *must* leave), and the worst thing we as parents can do is fail to prepare them to go because we have allowed them to skate through life without reaping what they sow. Our kids will spend most of their lives as adults, running their own lives: that's what we do, and we should parent with this reality in mind.

Forcing ourselves to think this way allows us to celebrate our kids for who they are, not who we want to manufacture them to be. It even allows us to celebrate and not covet our kids' classmates' gifts and talents. It gives us an opportunity to teach our children that life is not about selfies. It's about so much more.

One of the great honors of my life, one of the things I treasure the most, has been watching my son grow up to be a Godly man and now a Godly husband. Spencer and I have a deep and close relationship. I am blessed beyond measure that my one and only son is also my closest guy friend. Having him ask me to be his best man at his wedding is truly one of the highlights of my life and something I will cherish forever.

I thought a lot about what I would say in my toast, what I wanted to convey and emphasize as he started the next chapter of his life as a married man. I didn't talk much about my son's accolades. Instead, I focused on the good stuff, like character, courage, resilience, faithfulness, honor, and grace—the stuff that matters, the stuff that lasts.

In the song "Cat's in the Cradle," Harry Chapin talks about his boy being just like him. Truth is, our kids will model who we are and what we do far more than what we say. Hope I got it right.

Chapter 16

Lean On Me

If you're having trouble, it's OK to ask for help.
—Charlie Brown

Bill Withers's song "Lean On Me," written in 1972, is often recognized as one of the all-time greats and the ultimate bro song. Back in my college fraternity days, we played this song to pictures and videos at retreats, year-end meetings, during pledge recruitment—you name it, this was always the go-to song for camaraderie. It just makes all of us want to connect in a way that is honest and vulnerable. It encourages us to have deep and lasting friendships with people we love, people we trust.

One of the big life lessons from the song is to swallow our pride. Pride is defined a number of ways but always with a basic theme of being "in love of one's own excellence" or, more casually, of "being puffed up" or "full of yourself."

Pride creates blind spots where we do not see ourselves the way we really are. Pride means that internally we highlight our attributes and minimize our deficiencies or, in some cases, ignore them altogether. As I mentioned earlier, if humility is the greatest virtue, then pride is the most dangerous vice, a trait that can easily lead us down a path of destruction if we don't have someone to check us. We must have people in our lives who hold us accountable, calling us out when we go rogue, and we need to be willing to swallow our pride and lean on them when we are struggling.

I think God wants us to lean on people so we stay on track, and I think He wants us to lean on Him for the same reason. The Bible addresses pride and the need to seek wisdom often in two of the most well-known verses, Proverbs 3:5–6: "Trust in the Lord with all your heart and lean not on your own understanding; in all your ways submit to him, and he will make your paths straight."

Or as Charlie Brown and Bill Withers remind us: It is OK to ask for help. It is OK to lean on somebody.

* * *

Years ago, when I was in the busy days of raising a young family, I was introduced to a young man attending college in Santa Barbara. He was from out of town and new to the community, and some mutual friends thought he and I should connect, that we would enjoy each other, and that I could serve as sort of a local mentor. We hit it off, both sharing a love of sports, economics, and our faith, and ended up having a regular dinner once every six weeks or so, during which we talked about just about everything.

Soon after graduating, Vicki and I attended his wedding. He married his high school sweetheart, and this beautiful young couple had a full life in front of them . . . until she wanted out. While I don't feel like it is necessary or appropriate to share all of the sordid details, she spent too much time in an unhealthy way with another guy and ultimately decided her marriage wasn't worth holding on to.

Bottom line: it is a dangerous and slippery slope to connect in unhealthy ways with people outside of our marriage, and having an affair (whether it be emotional or physical) with someone other than your spouse always leads to dark and destructive consequences.

The two of us spent a fair amount of time talking during this difficult time, usually on his ride home from work. His heart was to pray for his marriage, that it would be redeemed and that he and his wife would be able to share their trial as a way to help others. But she had other plans, and before too long, their divorce was final. In this regard, the saying "It takes two" is nonsense. It takes one, only one, to destroy something that is good and beautiful.

Fortunately, this wasn't the end of the story for him, as in time he met a wonderful young lady who is an awesome person and perfect for him. Eventually, they got married and now have three children and a wonderful life together, full of love, joy, and purpose.

* * *

My dear friend in the story above was a casualty of his spouse behaving poorly, a trial he handled with character, grace, and resolve. Unfortunately, I have also witnessed the opposite, where people I know, in some cases people I love, blow up a marriage and a family in search of more money, more sex, or more excitement. "More, more, more—the grass is greener over there or with so and so" carries with it a lifetime of consequences and at the core is all about self over others.

For many of these episodes, Vicki and I were in the bleachers, afar, and not in a position to do much other that pray and hope, but for a few we were up close and personal in a place that allowed us (maybe even required us) to step into the messiness and try to help.

The crazy thing is how quickly people who should know better slid from someone solid, someone trustworthy, to someone who lost all sense of responsibility, all sense of right and wrong. In many cases, those who fell were the least likely of suspects, while in other cases, upon reflection, I could see the signs. Regardless, none of us should think this can only happen to the other guy or gal. We all must stay alert to the fact that all of us can fall and fall hard.

In each of my "interventions," I tried to show the love I have for my friends, while also not giving them a pass for bad behavior and things that just aren't right or appropriate. I can't help but think that in each of these cases, all the ugliness could have been avoided if they'd decided to swallow their pride and lean on me, lean on someone, lean on God.

* * *

There is a line at the end of the movie *The Usual Suspects* where Kevin Spacey's character, Keyser Söze, says, "The greatest trick the Devil ever pulled was convincing the world he didn't exist." Two footnotes before I continue: First, this movie would get zero stars for family friendliness because of bad language and violence. Second, if you haven't seen the movie and plan to, I just gave you way too much information—sorry. But seriously, we have got to be on the lookout for anything that can trip us up and cause us to lose our way.

In one of his many essays, Oswald Chambers writes about being aware of the least likely temptations. In other words, it is often the things that seem to be the most innocent and nonthreatening that lead us down a path of self-destruction. He is reminding us to be on high alert and avoid behavior or circumstances that can cause us to stray from our spouses, our kids, and our foundation.

This idea of a solid foundation is a really big deal because, as C. S. Lewis wrote, "Good and evil both increase at compound interest. That is why the little decisions you and I make every day are of such infinite importance. The smallest good act today is the capture of a strategic point from which, a few months later, you may be able to go on to victories you never dreamed of." And, of course, vice versa. The truth is, we are conformed to anything we say yes to.

* * *

I love the phrase "Barstow friend." For those who have never heard of Barstow, it's a small town about two hundred miles from Santa Barbara, kind of in the middle of nowhere, a simple, small place you pass while on your way to Mammoth Mountain to go skiing or on your way to Las Vegas. A Barstow friend is someone who on a Friday afternoon would drop everything and drive hours to Barstow to pick you up if you were in trouble.

Hopefully, we all have a few "Barstow friends" in our lives. And hopefully, we are a "Barstow friend" to others.

Sometimes I feel like I am a really good Barstow friend, but other times not so much. And it isn't just about getting in a car and sitting in traffic for hours to help out a buddy. It's about being available even when it is not super convenient or easy. It's about standing up for what's right or for those who are persecuted when it is not popular or when it costs us something. It's even about helping those who don't want our help.

In the case of my friends who went astray, it meant risking a friendship to stand up for what was good, what was honorable. It meant stepping in and stepping up to protect their families and try and help them get back on track.

Let us never forget that we all need somebody to lean on.

Chapter 17

Don't Worry, Be Happy

No worries, mate.
—Crocodile Dundee

For all you trivia buffs, here is a fun fact: The catchy tune "Don't Worry, Be Happy" is not an original Bob Marley song, and while the famous reggae artist may have sung it on occasion, it was originally written, composed, and sung by American musician Bobby McFerrin back in 1988, a year when it earned many awards, including Song of the Year. The vibe of the song does sound a lot like Bob Marley and is consistent with the name and main chorus, "Don't worry, be happy," which seem like pretty good words to live by.

When our kids were little, we got turned on to this secluded little island in the West Indies as the ultimate chill vacation spot. I realize this sounds a bit extravagant and far away, but we never really minded the challenges of traveling with three little kids, mostly because my wife is the master of distraction and figured out ways to keep them engaged throughout the airplane rides and downtime at the airports.

The island, while being super cool, was also understated and simple, with one small resort and a sampling of homes both on the beach and in the hills overlooking the water. No cars allowed: just golf carts (or mules, as the locals call them) to get around, a small, neighborhood-style grocery store, a fish market (which was really just fish in coolers on the beach), a couple of restaurants, and an ice cream shop that became part of our daily routine.

One day while cruising into the store to grab some snacks, there was an old, frayed piece of paper taped to the bulletin board behind the counter that caught my eye. The board was not organized and consisted of photos and some notes, both thank-yous from guests and orders placed for pickup from people staying on the island. It was the color of this piece of paper that was notebook size and haphazardly placed near the middle of the board that got my attention. It had a bright yellow background, and the words were printed with vivid green letters, which was fitting for the Caribbean vibe. And then at the top, the header that read "Strive to be happy" in a font that was much bigger than anything else.

I asked the young lady behind the counter if I could take a closer look, and with her permission, I read the text and took a picture, which, like most photos in a predigital world, probably lies in a box in a closet somewhere.

Doing some research when I got home, I learned that the words were taken from a poem written by Max Ehrmann called "Desiderata," which means "something that is needed or wanted." The poem is written almost like advice from a life coach, or with one of those Life is Good T-shirts or stickers in mind.

These days, you can find the words to "Desiderata" in a variety of formats online: check 'em out, there is some good wisdom there. The poem moves from one point to another and is not necessarily cohesive but has a certain charm to it along with some valuable lessons, before ending with a reminder that despite life being hard, the world is still a beautiful place.

One of our family vacation traditions is to bring back a map, a picture, or something else that really captures the place we are visiting. This is not unique to the Dusebout family, as I am sure most families bring back knickknacks and such when on vacation. In this case, I thought the bright colors and uplifting message would be a cool memento to bring home, so I asked if there was another copy that I could buy.

"Oh, Mr. Drew, I'm not sure. This has been here for a long time. I know it was here before I first came to the island ten years ago."

I love the fact that this place was small enough that people got to know our names, and I especially love the fact that no one even tried to tackle our last name: it was just Mr. Drew. This is pretty much the way it goes throughout my life—this is the curse or blessing, depending on your point of view, of having a last name that no one can pronounce.

Sensing I had an interest in local culture and a spiritual side to me, she said, "We have a church service every Sunday, and you and your family are welcome to join us if you would like."

My general view when traveling is to find time to get to know the local culture and people and church is often a good way to make that happen. So, at 8 a.m. that Sunday, wearing our best island clothes (which meant pressed shorts for me and my son, and summer dresses for the girls), we arrived at an older building atop a hill where there was a community of small homes.

I learned these were homes to many of those who worked on the island. The setting was great, but there was clearly a sharp contrast between these places and the homes where we and the vacationers stayed. The church was painted in bright colors but lacked the finishes and richness of the chapel in "town" where weddings happened, or where the occasional celebrity visitor would read stories at Christmas or Easter.

We were greeted by a large group of local folks, with all the men wearing suits and the women dressed in bright colors. My wife always feels like our family and Americans in general are sloppy and too informal, but for me, I'll live with the casual look, as the thought of wearing a suit or even long pants in the heat with no air conditioning is not all that appealing. Regardless of the fact that we stood out because of our attire as well as the color of our skin, we were welcomed like long-lost friends with smiles and hugs. We were escorted to a bench near the front of the church and handed a hymn book, then treated to some wonderful gospel music, after which a pastor who had a sweet way about her talked about all the different church activities and led us into more singing.

About an hour and a half in, my girls needed to use the restroom, so Vicki quietly took them outside to both go to the bathroom and stretch their legs. My son, who is the oldest, was eight, and he was struggling to sit still (can't blame him, as it is hard to sit anywhere for that long at his age, even more so in the intense heat). I was enjoying the experience but also realized that we weren't going to make it much longer, so I sat trying to figure out how to leave without offending anyone. Sensing my challenge, a young man walked up the aisle and leaned in toward me. Turns out, he was the waiter that had served us fries and soft drinks the day before and explained, "Church here is not like your church back home. We start at 8 a.m. but we finish whenever God wants us to—sometimes at noon, sometimes not until dinnertime. Please do not feel like you have to stay. We rarely get vacationers, and it was wonderful that you came. Come on, let me walk you outside where our lead pastor is praying. I know he wants to meet you."

Thankful for his intervention, we walked outside, where we met the pastor. He was a big man with a deep voice, kind of like James Earl Jones in the movies. He gave us all a hug (lots of huggers on the island) and told me he had something for me. He mentioned that I had met his niece in the store and asked about the poem behind the counter. He said he was able to find another one in a storage room and that he wanted me to have it. Unlike the one in the store, this sheet of paper was rolled up all nice with a plastic wrapping around it.

Feeling a bit embarrassed, I told him I really appreciated the gesture, but he certainly did not need to give this to us. Why not replace the old paper, which was hanging by a thread, with this newer one? He responded with words that have really stuck with me, words that really define the way we all should live. He said, "Mr. Drew"—always Mr.

Drew—"please don't rob me of my blessing." In essence, he got joy out of doing this, and while I was the one who got something tangible, it was he who received something more important.

I nodded and accepted his gift and asked about his sermon for the day, adding that we were going to head out, as the kids were restless. He thanked me, which once again seemed like it should have been the other way around, and said he understood it is hard to sit in church with small children for very long.

He then told me that today, he'd teaching from the Book of Matthew, specifically Matthew 6:25–27: "Therefore I tell you, do not worry about your life, what you will eat or drink; or about your body, what you will wear. Is not life more than food, and the body more than clothes? Look at the birds of the air; they do not sow or reap or store away in barns, and yet your heavenly Father feeds them. Are you not much more valuable than they? Can any one of you by worrying add a single hour to your life?"

I thought about this—do not worry about your life—in the context of him just standing outside chatting with us, not worried about the schedule or agenda inside the church and how much different this is at home, where every minute of our church service and most things for that matter are planned and organized. I got the sense that he looked at us and all of the other people who came to the island with money, sometimes lots of it, and the hectic schedules and complex balance sheets that typically go with a life of affluence, with a sort of sadness.

There is a certain contentment to the people living on this island and many people who live in what we in America call the developing parts of the world that we can learn from. In a way, it's a strange paradigm—at times we may feel sorry for them because they lack many of the physical comforts that we take for granted, and at times I think they feel sorry for us because we always seem so stressed out, preoccupied, and unable to find contentment without all our stuff.

They actually live by the words "Don't worry, be happy." Wouldn't that be nice?

* * *

This idea of "don't worry, be happy" plays its way into our society through the entertainment industry in a variety of ways. Australian native Paul Hogan's character Crocodile Dundee made "No worries, mate" a staple of casual conversation in America back in the 1980s when the film came out, and of course, for those of us with kids, it is hard not to chime in when hearing "Hakuna Matata" from *The Lion King*, which was taken from a Swahili phrase meaning "no problems." I can still picture the animated characters Timon and Pumba dancing around and singing to that simple and "hard to get out of your mind" melody.

The Bible weighs in on this topic of worry a whole bunch of times as well, including in one of my favorite verses from the Book of Philippians. "Be anxious for nothing, but in everything by prayer and supplication, with thanksgiving, let your requests be made known to God; and the peace of God, which surpasses all understanding, will guard your hearts and minds through Christ Jesus" (Phil. 4:6–7).

Think about how the author, the Apostle Paul, one of the heroes of the Christian faith, encourages us to be "anxious for nothing." He tells us to go to God and pray, making our needs known, and that by doing this, we will receive a peace that exceeds all our expectations. He is reminding us that God will provide us with joy even in the midst of our trials, even when our lives don't turn out the way we want.

A while back, while enjoying a few days of rest at a safari camp near the border between Kenya and Tanzania, my family and I had an opportunity to spend some time visiting a traditional Maasai village where the families lived in small huts put together by a combination of straw, grass, and cow dung. There were a handful of huts in one area protected by a fence made out of sticks to keep the lions and other predators away from their livestock, and a cluster of these areas in close proximity to one another formed a small village or neighborhood.

After getting out of our jeep and walking around for a bit, we were invited to sit inside one of the huts to have some coffee with a mom and her children. It was a fascinating experience and one that forced me to quickly adapt and get over my mild case of claustrophobia. The huts themselves were really small and dark, with a few rooms separated by more of the same straw, grass, and dung that make up the exterior walls. They were short, so short that you had to crouch to enter and stay crouched or sitting once inside. We got settled cross-legged on the dirt floor, and the mom served us coffee while we visited with the help of our guide, Samson, who was proficient in both English and the local Maasai dialect.

One of the girls who sat alongside us was about the same age as my daughters and dressed in traditional Maasai garb, full of bright colors and jewelry. Knowing that we were interested in the water aspect of their lives, Sembui showed us the bucket that she strapped to her back when she set off for the well to get water.

We learned that she walked to get water pretty much every day, so we decided to go with her to get the complete local experience. Samson carried a spear for protection, which in a way made us feel safe, and in another way made us feel like we were sitting ducks. We took turns carrying the bucket, both empty on the three-mile trek there and full on the way back.

Sembui was quite talkative and seemed happy. She did not seem particularly concerned that she was missing out on a better life. Maybe because her life is all she knows, but as Samson shared, the Maasai are generally happy people, content to live a simple nomadic life. He reminded us that as we in the West come to help, come to protect them and their land (which, for the most part, is a good thing), we also need to respect their way of life, even learn from it.

Sometimes simple means less worrying; sometimes simple means more happiness.

"Don't worry, be happy."

Chapter 18

G.G.

I do not believe one can settle how much we ought to give. I am afraid the only safe rule is to give more than we can spare.
—C. S. Lewis

"Lonely People" is a best-selling song written by Dan and Catherine Peek. Dan, along with Dewey Bunnell and Gerry Beckley, was one of the three original members of America, a band that was popular back in the 1970s for its close vocal harmonies and light acoustic folk-rock sound.

Perhaps not so well known is that many of Peek's compositions have deep and spiritual undertones to them, with a perspective of seeking and longing for something bigger than ourselves. "Lonely People," a call for the lonely and despairing to seek God, is one of these songs and easily his most well known.

Myrtle, or G.G., as my kids often called her (as an abbreviated nickname for great-grandmother), spent a good portion of her life living alone. Her first husband, Burnell, passed away when he was quite young, and years later, she was married to Stan, who was a pastor, for a short time before he, too, passed away.

Yet, even as a widow, any time we visited her, we found her kitchen table was set for two. "One seat for me and one seat for Jesus," she would say with just a touch of a Southern accent that came from being born and raised in Texas. "You see, you're never alone when you have the Lord."

Back in the 1970s and '80s, the sitcom *Happy Days* was a huge hit that provided an idealistic view of life in the midwestern United States from the mid-1950s to the mid-1960s. There is a particular episode that takes place on Christmas Eve in which Fonzie, the cool biker character played by Henry Winkler, wishes everyone at the local diner a Merry Christmas and then heads back to his apartment, which doubles as his garage, and opens a can of ravioli to heat up on a hot plate.

Watching the guy who always gets the girl and is tough enough that all the guys look up to him in awe sit by himself on Christmas Eve eating canned food is sad and not what we as viewers expect. He's supposed to be somewhere fun, somewhere we would all want to be. Because this was generally a happy show, no pun intended, Fonzie is ultimately "rescued" by his buddy Richie Cunningham and the Cunningham family, who serve as the innocent, "too good to be true" all-American family throughout the life of the series, and he ends up spending Christmas Eve with them.

But the show does make a point about this idea of loneliness. It is a real thing, and sometimes the lonely are not who we think they are. When our lives are full of kids, work, and activity, we can all long for some alone time. But for those people in society who are by themselves (the elderly, the homeless, the broken), it is a source of pain and despair. I just don't think we as human beings are meant to do life solo. I feel like God made us in a way that we long for companionship, and all of us should remember this when we think about the widows and the orphans, those without family or friends. We should all do more for the lonely people. And if we find ourselves lonely, maybe Myrtle is onto something. Setting a table for two seems like a pretty good idea.

* * *

Myrtle Belland was born in Comanche, Texas, on October 16, 1912. Comanche is a tiny, rural town even by small-town standards, and she was raised as a Texas cowgirl before moving to Los Angeles with her husband, Burnell, in her early twenties. After Burnell died, being a hard worker and fiercely independent, she took a job as a cashier in the radiology department at UCLA, where she worked up until the time she retired.

Myrtle was very much a lady while at the same time being tough as nails. She was definitely someone who liked to dress nice. Living in Santa Barbara, I show up to the family barbeque in a T-shirt, shorts, and flip-flops. Myrtle would show up dressed to the nines with jewelry, makeup, the whole nine yards.

But Myrtle was also tough. When we first moved to Santa Barbara twenty-three years ago, we rented a home that had a short breezeway from the garage to the house. One afternoon, Vicki, Myrtle, and our son, Spencer, who was all of six months old, were leaving the garage. Vicki was leading with Spencer in her arms when she encountered a rattlesnake nestled in the corner of the breezeway. My wife, terrified of snakes, darted into the house. Myrtle, as dressed up as always, yelled out: "Vicki, dear, where is a shovel or hoe?" She found the hoe, and with her purse tucked under one arm, cut the snake right in half. Waiting until the snake stopped moving (snakes move even after their head is cut off), she picked up both pieces of the snake and threw them into the bushes, then walked inside looking like a million bucks with her purse still under her arm and said, "Let's have a nice cup of tea."

Myrtle was cool, Myrtle was tough, and she did love her tea.

Starting when she was in her late twenties during the Depression era, Myrtle, along with some of her friends, became involved in the King's Daughters (KDs for short) Los Angeles Chapter. (Technically it's called The King's Daughters and Sons, but I leave the sons off because if we are honest, us guys do little of the work). KD's is a Christian organization based in upstate New York with chapters around the United States and Canada that does good work for others.

Myrtle had a deep faith and was the spiritual head of our family up until she passed away at the ripe old age of ninety-nine. Her love for God and unwavering commitment to serving Him led her and a small group of ladies to give whatever they could to the KDs, even during tough times. Sometimes she could only give $1 a week, needing the rest of her meager paycheck to help put food on the table. Other times, she was able to give more, but she and her friends always gave and gave more than they could spare, sacrificially and putting God's economy first.

Eventually, Myrtle became the leader of the Los Angeles chapter, during which time the KDs owned and operated a home in West Los Angeles, a home that served elderly ladies who were widowed or unmarried and needed companionship and a little help with the necessities of life.

As she got older, she just couldn't serve any longer, and the next generation of potential KD leaders had other interests, so with some help, she sold the home to a school, thus helping children in the area. Because real estate in West Los Angeles is valuable, the proceeds from the sale ended up being quite a bit of money. Myrtle was never a wealthy woman in the traditional sense of the word. She was independent and comfortable as a result of living within her means, but certainly not affluent. Because she was used to adhering to a budget and from the Depression era, Myrtle held on to those funds like she did her purse: tightly, waiting for direction from God to guide her on what to do.

I think Matthew 25:21 sums up this part of Myrtle's journey: "His master replied, 'Well done, good and faithful servant! You have been faithful with a few things; I will put you in charge of many things.'" The faithfulness of the small gifts made by Myrtle and her friends had multiplied to a fair sum of money, over 1.5 million dollars, and now God entrusted Myrtle to steward it.

At first, some of the other KDs leaders pressured her to send the money back to KDs headquarters, as it was too much money and over their heads. But Myrtle stood steadfast, believing that God had entrusted her to oversee these resources,

While I know that she felt strongly that God wanted her to watch over this money, I also know that, at times, this assignment was a burden to her. As much as she got the giving and saving part of money right, she had a hard time with the spending part. It wasn't that Myrtle wanted more for herself; it was just growing up in the Depression, she was practical and thrifty, and this sum of money was overwhelming. It was important for her to get this right, and her lack of tangible action for a season should not be interpreted as her being lazy or disinterested, but rather a sign of her commitment to patiently and prayerfully wait for God to lead her.

This ongoing diligence and discernment eventually led her to Vicki. Myrtle was Vicki's grandmother, or nana as my wife called her, but their relationship was much more than that. Vicki and Myrtle were tight, the closest of friends, and as Vicki and I grew in our faith and stewardship, Myrtle noticed the change in us and at some point became comfortable enough to ask Vicki (with an assist from me) to head up the KDs Los Angeles Chapter and help invest the capital—not in stocks and bonds, mind you, but in things with eternal significance.

Honored to be a part of this, collectively we have been able to use these funds to bless a number of organizations, including the Children's Hospital of Los Angeles; the Corporate Chaplains of America; ELMO (the Christian school that her great-grandchildren Spencer, Jessie, and Dani attended); Acres of Love, which operates homes for orphaned children in South Africa; and Hands4Others, whose mission is to rise up young leaders to help solve the world's water crisis.

There is a great lesson here. Saying "yes" to something meaningful even in small ways can lead to some really big things that literally change the world. Something that started small with sacrificial gifts of as little as $1 per week and modest ambition eventually helped save the lives of thousands of children clear across the world, children that Myrtle or the other KDs leaders will never meet this side of Heaven.

I think about how lucky I am to get a glimpse of all this, and as an investment guy, I always try my best to remember that it's hard to find a better ROI than from an investment made with helping others in mind. And I always try to be a little more like Myrtle each day.

When Myrtle passed away at the ripe age of ninety-nine, I had the honor to share a few words both in Santa Barbara at a memorial service here and in Comanche, where she was buried next to her beloved Burnell, wearing her fur coat, favorite jewelry, and all. Before I spoke, I thought about her life, and couldn't help but settle in on this passage from James 2:17: "In the same way, faith by itself, if it is not accompanied by action, is dead."

Myrtle—thank you for living your faith out loud in a way that blessed others. Our memories of you provoke tears, laughter, and gratitude, and always will. Till we see each other again!

Chapter 19

Catch and Release

No one has ever become poor by giving.
—Anne Frank

For us fly-fishers, catch and release means we land the giant trout, get her in the net, take a picture to hang on the wall and secure bragging rights with our friends, and then revive the fish and let her go, healthy and vibrant for the next angler lucky enough or skilled enough to catch.

To paraphrase the words of my buddy Ian, "catch and release" in life means to hold on loosely to the stuff we earn, the stuff we are fortunate enough to grab onto, to accept what we receive, and avoid the temptation to keep it or hoard it for ourselves, but rather let it go to help others. God invites us to an adventure in generosity if we let Him.

There are many ways to soak in and be challenged by this theme of generosity. Ian, me, and four other guys, who have become a band of brothers, have made a point to gather on a regular basis and do some fun and crazy stuff, like paraglide off the top of Rendezvous Mountain in Jackson Hole, float and camp on the Snake River, and hike our way beyond marked trails to explore caves. But amid the adrenaline, we also go deep emotionally and spiritually. We spend much of our time talking about our blessings and what it looks like to release them. We encourage

one another to live by the words the Apostle Paul spoke in Acts 20:35—
"It is more blessed to give than receive"—and give away what we own,
which I am pretty sure all belongs to God in the first place.

In a much more formal way than a week of craziness with my friends,
a few years ago I found myself with a group of strangers at a conference,
an experience that perfectly exemplifies the saying "Never say never."

My three golden rules are as follows:

1. I don't do cruises.
2. I try to avoid buffets (except for breakfast).
3. I never attend events that require name tags.

Some people love cruises, which is fine—different strokes for different folks—and for years, my kids always wanted to go on a Disney
cruise, which they are welcome to do someday when they have their
own kids. Maybe I will cave on this with my grandkids, but so far, I've
stayed strong.

Buffets were great back in the day when I was broke and on a tight
budget and didn't have to worry about calories. Shakey's Pizza was my
favorite, with unlimited fried chicken, pizza, and salad with all the
blue cheese dressing you could pile on. But I think it was a restaurant
on one of my kids' school trips where the roast beef and Jell-O tasted
the same that ruined it for me.

Name tags mean I have forced visits with people I do not know. I
am generally an extroverted person, but for some reason, the thought
of mingling in this manner is not appealing.

All of these idiosyncrasies lead me to be a person who generally
does not attend conferences. So, when my friend Jim invited Vicki
and me to attend a Generous Giving conference, or G.G. conference
as Vicki nicknamed it, my first instinct was to say, "Thanks, but no
thanks." But for some reason, in this case, I felt like I was supposed to
say "yes," and the next thing I knew, we were in Scottsdale, Arizona,
violating two of my three golden rules.

It is important for me to point out that I am not implying that Jim invited me because I was or am a generous giver. I think it is far more likely that he invited so I would become a generous giver. He was just too polite to say so.

* * *

I know the comparison game is wrong and can lead to a life of jealousy and misery, but at some level most of us cannot help ourselves. *When it comes to money, I am more generous than so and so*; *Boy, those people sure do herd their stuff*, and *Aren't they cheap?* are thoughts that have crept into my mind. If you are suffering from this same ailment, I have the cure: go to a Generous Giving conference because after sitting in that room and listening to story after story of lives of abundance and generosity, I was both inspired and convicted. I was no longer looking at my less generous friends. I was looking at myself. I remember whispering to Vicki at one point, telling her that I felt like everyone was looking at us, saying, "There they are: that's the selfish couple Jim invited." Obviously, that wasn't the case, but I did feel like if the tables were set up by levels of giving, I would be at the back of the room, maybe even in the hallway.

The people were wonderful, as one might expect at a conference based on generosity, and I actually came to respect, if not fully appreciate, the name tags.

As mentioned, we heard many encouraging stories about giving and met some great people over those few days. We talked with people who were being advised about how to creatively give away their investment properties, personal residences, and other illiquid assets so their resources could be used to help others—now, not later, after they have died.

This is one of the reasons I am generally against large savings accounts and endowments. Why hold the money when you can use it for good now? As a finance guy, I understand the practice of an organization holding six months of operating expenses in case there is a revenue shortfall or a family having some savings for a rainy day or retirement, but how much is enough? Do top universities really need $10, $20, or even $30 billion endowments? Do we really need to retire young and rich, living a life without real purpose?

That was the beauty of this conference. No one who presented or I met was thinking this way. Play the comparison game in this crowd and you will end up with a smaller wallet.

One of the stories that stuck with me was from a family who owned a large industrial company and made the decision to live a comfortable, modest life while giving away most of their substantial profits. Ultimately they gave away the entire company, maintaining a 1 percent interest so they could continue to operate it. I remember listening to the story—and this is by memory and these numbers are to the best of my recollection, so do not hold me to them, but I am certainly in the ballpark—of how they lived on something like three times the poverty level or $165,000 per year and gave over $1,000,000 away. I was thinking, *Wow, that is crazy generous*, only to find out that they were not giving away $1,000,000 per year—they were giving away $1,000,000 per *month*. Seriously, I have never heard of such a thing, and I thought our giving a growing percentage of our income was huge.

But even more than their level of giving, it was the words of one of the sons in the family who spoke that really made me think. He was not bitter or upset that his parents gave away his inheritance. He was grateful for the lessons and blessings that he and his siblings had experienced through the generous giving of his folks. It wasn't his money anyway, he told us, it was entrusted to his parents and ultimately belonged to God.

Now, the comparison game is no fun at all, and I got to thinking about how my kids can be spoiled at times, and how Vicki and I spoil them ourselves. I got to thinking about the heirs to great wealth who are robbed from building their own lives and instead spend time and energy looking back and trying to hold on to their family's legacy and money instead of moving forward. And I got to thinking about the really rich families out there who often end up dysfunctional, estranged, and suing one another wanting more. Seems like in the case of money, less really is more. Maybe we all should learn to catch and release.

Chapter 20

Everything?

Mama says, "Stupid is as stupid does."
—Forrest Gump

Early in my career, thirty-plus years ago, I found myself a leader of small but growing, lucrative business, a niche business that I stumbled onto and was lucky enough to recognize and get after. As things got going, I ended up working with a couple of business partners who were my friends long before we started making a living together. On paper, everything was cool: work hard, make some money, and hang out.

Except that's not how things went. As young guys new to success, we were all a bit full of ourselves, and I am pretty sure I was the ringleader in terms of less-than-stellar behavior. Without much mentorship in my life up until that point, I was at times hard to get along with, bossy and arrogant, thinking that was the way leadership was supposed to look. Spoiler alert—despite what we might see at times in the business world, in politics, or on TV, it's not.

Life is messy, people are messy (which really means I'm messy), partnerships are messy, and it takes humility all around to make them last. As I struggled, knowing things couldn't continue the way they were, eventually I made my way to Carl, a friend and another one of my unsung heroes who spent years helping me figure life out.

He gave me a book written by Ken Sande called *The Peacemaker: A Biblical Guide to Resolving Personal Conflict*. Every time I would come back to Carl and express my frustration with my circumstances, he'd ask, "Did you read the book I gave you?" I would say something to the effect of, "No, but here is what is happening and here is what I am doing." He would just look at me with an expression that matched the words of Forrest Gump's mom, an expression that said, "Stupid is as stupid does—you really are dense." Thankfully, he was patient with me, and at the end of the day I think he gave me three copies of the same book to try and make his point: read it, dummy. In desperation I finally picked it up and started reading. It took all of ten pages for me to go "Uh oh," and another couple of chapters for me to realize that everything (yes, everything) I was doing to try and remedy things was wrong.

I was focused on winning and being right rather than solving and getting it right.

* * *

Late one summer night when I was twelve years old, my friend Kent's dad shared with me and my friend one of these valuable life lessons. Being a college professor, he had a slow, steady, deliberate style of instruction, a style that sometimes made us squirm with impatience, as we just wanted him to get to the point. I think it was because he was an intellectual used to teaching college students and we were young and not yet serious about life. But on this night, he used a line from a famous poem to try and subtly get through to us, and for some reason it has always stuck in the back of my mind. "The best laid schemes o' Mice an' Men / Gang aft agley" is taken from the poem "To a Mouse," written by Robert Burns in 1785, and translates into English as "The best-laid plans of mice and men often go awry," meaning no matter how carefully plans are made, no matter how much we think we know what we are doing, sometimes we just don't get it right.

Growing up in the suburbs outside of Seattle, I spent a fair amount of time at my friend's summerhouse on Whidbey Island, which was a short ferry ride from the mainland. It was an idyllic way to spend a summer: riding bikes and exploring the rugged topography and beaches that provided clams, oysters, and large beds of sand dollars. I hate to sound cliché or like I am trying to write a Pat Conroy or John Irving novel, but it was a simpler, safer time, and we could pretty much roam about without fear or much supervision.

The sun sets late in Seattle in the summer. So, one evening at dusk, about 9 p.m., we decided it would be a good idea to take the guts from the fish we'd caught, hop in my friend's rickety old rowboat, row out past the kelp beds, and churn the water with the fish guts, hoping to attract little sharks around the boat, which we could then catch or just watch them frenzy.

This was the summer when the movie *Jaws* was released, and I think we were intrigued by the idea of seeing sharks and proving that we were macho, unaffected by the fears that gripped much of the nation that summer. The anxiety from the movie was both irrational and extreme. I even remember my sister and her friends refusing to go swimming in our pool because of sharks, and being the loving big brother that I am, I coaxed them to finally jump in one night and then quickly turned off the pool lights, provoking hysteria and screams (told you the fear of sharks was both irrational and extreme).

Shifting back to my time on the rowboat: our plan worked perfectly until it didn't. We churned the fish guts, and little sharks and dogfish showed up and frenzied. It was awesome . . . until our oarlocks broke, and the current began to take us away from the shore and down the beach. Rowing without oarlocks is not as easy or fruitful as rowing with them. I suppose that is why there are oarlocks in the first place, but regardless, we couldn't get any leverage to stop us from drifting. We tried standing up, but the boat was small, old, and unstable.

Suddenly, we weren't so tough, as the thought of falling into the water after just watching sharks frenzy kept us in our seats.

Now with the sky pitch black, we bounced back and forth, not literally in the boat (as the ocean wasn't that rough), but emotionally as we went from still thinking that our adventure was really cool to realizing we were in deep trouble. The beach parallel to our boat was shaped like a half-moon, with the tip of it jutting out like a small peninsula, while beyond the point was open water, shipping lanes, and Canada.

We thought about our options: just stay in the boat and hopefully be rescued at some point, as there had to be a ton of big ships in the open water. We nixed that plan, realizing it was dark and that without any light on board, we were more likely to be run over than found.

Ultimately, and I can still hear the theme song from *Jaws* playing in my head, we hopped into the water, grabbed the rope tied to the front of the boat, and starting swimming to shore, taking turns pulling the boat with us. Our plan was to ground the boat and ourselves at that point, not wanting to return home "boatless" and in trouble. The boat was probably worth fifty bucks in 1975 dollars, yet most of our discussion was about how to save it; you would have thought it was a yacht or expensive sailboat.

I love to swim, and I love the ocean, but there's nothing tranquil about swimming in dark, cold water at night, especially with visions of sharks in your head. We stuck together, figuring if the sharks did come, two of us would have a better chance than one of us (great wisdom), and because it just didn't seem fair for one of us to race ahead of whoever was pulling the boat.

To put a stop to the suspense, we did make it to shore, broken boat and all, and didn't even have to fend off any sea creatures on the way.

Cold and wet, we headed back along the beach, full of adrenaline and goosebumps. Shivering in part from fear and part because we were freezing, we half-walked and half-ran down the beach, spending most of our time either talking about how we escaped death or trying to figure out how we were going to explain all this to his parents.

Arriving home in the wee hours of the night, we walked into the house to find his mother frantic, not hysterical, but certainly worried, and his father calm and perplexed. Not to harp on this theme that "it was a different time or era," but I'm quite sure that if this happened today, police would have been called in, Amber Alerts would have been issued, and the worst feared.

After we took a warm shower and got some food, I remember my friend's dad looking over his glasses and asking us in an inquisitive manner what on earth happened. I think he was smoking a pipe during our discussion but admit this just may be the way I want to remember things versus what really happened. Nevertheless, it does provide a decent image of the setting. He was a good listener and after allowing us the time to ramble on about our tale, exaggerating and sensationalizing things just a bit, he pointed out in a scholarly, not angry, manner that "the best-laid plans of mice and men often go awry"—that as much we thought we had devised the perfect plan, we had pretty much got everything wrong.

And thirty-plus years ago, that is exactly what Carl was also trying to tell me. As a leader, I had it all wrong.

* * *

Getting it right requires a pause at times, a speed check in which we stop and listen to that little voice inside us all that I'm quite sure comes from God when He's trying to get our attention, as well as the voice of others whom we trust, those who have our best interests at heart. We need to be willing to reset and change our direction, if need be, rather than stubbornly holding onto a predetermined path.

Annie Duke's book *Thinking in Bets* does a good job of making this point with real-life illustrations as the author talks about the merits in an uncertain world of embracing the concept of "I am not sure."

She shares that many of us grab hold of a truth, dig in, and rarely change our minds, even when the facts clearly show we are wrong.

In short, we convince ourselves of a certain narrative and reinforce it over and over, thus making compromise, conflict resolution, and getting to the best decision nearly impossible.

Don't believe me? Isn't this what happens in the political arena, where leaders on all sides refuse to give in, refuse to give an inch, solely for the sake of winning? Look at how they treat those with whom they disagree, the consequences of angry and divisive rhetoric, and how those in charge seek self and power instead of civility and service. Anybody find this appealing or helpful?

Better to listen, better to change our minds when it makes sense and lead with a soft heart alongside a thoughtful mind. Said differently, if we can learn to talk about the tough stuff rationally in the same tone we use when we are talking about the weather without a hard heart and a bunch of baggage and emotion, we are much more likely to make good decisions and treat people well, which, by the way, should go hand in hand.

* * *

Mother Teresa once said, "I used to believe that prayer changes things, but now I know that prayer changes us and we change things," and as a prayerful person, I get what she is saying. Prayer softens our hearts and help us see issues and people from another perspective. It's the opposite of becoming entrenched in one point of view and allows us to connect to others in healthy ways, valuing them even when we are at odds or feel slighted.

Here's my big takeaway: disagreements are part of life, and in many cases, there isn't a clear wrong or right answer, one that is for sure better than the others. Rather, there is a clear and right way to behave, a path in which we do the right thing and act the right way regardless of circumstances or how others are behaving, one in which we are quick to forgive and equally as quick to ask for forgiveness.

I still remember, after Carl finally got me to listen to him and read Ken Sande's book, when I knew that I needed to apologize to my partners, a real apology that was sincere and genuine rather than one with an agenda. This was a different kind of apology (and has to be if we really want to get along) than the half-baked apologies that are far more common in our culture, ones that start with an "I'm sorry, but . . . ," which is really a not-so-subtle way of saying you got what you deserve masked with trite and meaningless platitudes.

Thankfully, they were agreeable, and I was given the chance to do better, to lead better. I was grateful and took the opportunity to heart, moving off my high horse and into a place that I think honored all involved. And while I am still a work in progress (we all are), I believe I'm heading in the right direction with the right motives.

Want to avoid "stupid does?" Want to make a difference for good? Be humble, keep listening, and change your mind more often than you think you need to. Trust me, from experience, it works a whole lot better than the other way around.

Chapter 21

You Serious, Clark?

Things work out best for those who make
the best of the way things work out.
—John Wooden

"You serious, Clark?" That line from *National Lampoon's Christmas Vacation* always gets me. For those who do not remember the line or inexcusably have never seen the movie, allow me to set the stage.

With the whole extended (and I mean really extended family) sitting at the dinner table on Christmas, Clark Griswold, played by Chevy Chase, tries to lighten the mood after a series of disasters by saying, "Hey, kids, I heard on the news that an airline pilot spotted Santa's sleigh on its way in from New York." After a pause, Eddie, who's a grown man and one of the funniest movie characters of all time, asks, "You serious, Clark?"

OK, so it's hard to deliver the punch line in writing, but for years, I have tortured my kids by responding to things they say with that line. It just cracks me up; I am easily amused.

In Rosamund Stone Zander and Benjamin Zander's best-selling book *The Art of Possibility*, they talk about what they call Rule Number 6 with the following story.

Two prime ministers are sitting in a room discussing affairs of state. Suddenly a man bursts in, apoplectic with fury, shouting and stamping and banging his fist on the desk. The resident prime minister admonishes him: "Peter," he says, "kindly remember Rule Number 6," whereupon Peter is instantly restored to complete calm, apologizes, and withdraws.

The politicians return to their conversation, only to be interrupted yet again twenty minutes later by a hysterical woman gesticulating wildly, her hair flying. Again, the intruder is greeted with the words "Marie, please remember Rule Number 6." Complete calm descends once more, and she, too, withdraws with a bow and an apology.

When the scene is repeated for a third time, the visiting prime minister addresses his colleague: "My dear friend, I've seen many things in my life, but never anything as remarkable as this. Would you be willing to share with me the secret of Rule Number 6?"

"Very simple," replies the resident prime minister. "Rule Number 6 is, 'Don't take yourself so damn seriously.'"

"Ah," says his visitor, "that is a fine rule." After a moment of pondering, he inquires, "And what, may I ask, are the other rules?"

"There aren't any."

In other words, chill out! Laugh a little!

* * *

The last chapter of my mom's life was spent in a nursing home a couple of miles from our house, which was nice, because we could stop by and visit her, even spontaneously when schedules permitted, and she was up and with it.

Because the place was highly regulated, I often received calls when something didn't go exactly right. The rules required the nurses to call a family member, in this case me, if something out of the ordinary happened. I got a fair number of calls. "Your mom's gums started to bleed when she brushed her teeth." "Your mom has a bruise on her arm from banging into a door." The calls were always thoughtful and respectful, and I wasn't too nervous when I saw the number from the facility light up on my phone. This was the new normal.

One day I got a call and picked up to the usual greeting that was always very formal: "Mr. Dusebout, this is so-and-so from the nursing home." But this time, the message was a bit different. "We are calling because today your mom got into an altercation with another one of our residents."

I remember thinking, *My mom is four feet ten inches tall and confined to a wheelchair. How the heck did she get into an altercation?* So, I asked the question that all of us want answered. Drum roll please . . .

"How did she do?"

"Excuse me, Mr. Dusebout, I don't understand what you mean."

Poor guy did not know how to deal with me.

I said, "My mother got in a fight. How did she do? Did she win?"

Sigh, pause, and then, "Well, the other lady is an ex–military officer and kind of rough. She did hit your mom in the face, who now has a small contusion under her eye, but when the other resident tried to take your mom's blanket, your mom grabbed hold of her hand and dug her fingernails in hard enough to draw a little blood and just wouldn't let go. We actually couldn't believe she was that strong and had to pry her hands off the other lady."

"OK, then," I said, "good news. My mom won on points."

Please don't think I am callous or insensitive to the condition my mom was in late in her life. It was sad and often broke my heart. But sometimes, as corny as it sounds, laughter truly is the best medicine. In this life, we will have trials, and we will have tragedy and setbacks. Faith and perspective allow us to find joy and even laugh a little in the midst of having a broken heart.

* * *

I tend to check out on airplanes. It is "my" time to read, think, binge-watch the series du jour, and sleep. Most people do the same. Walk onto an airplane these days and you will likely see the majority of people with headphones on and a portable electronic device out—even during takeoff and landing—or eyes closed, isolated from everyone around them. But, if we think about it, airplanes are perhaps the most prolific of all places to meet people. Where else are we all stuck with one another in close quarters for hours with nowhere to go?

A few years ago, Vicki and I were on a plane traveling from Colorado to Los Angeles. There were two sets of three seats on each side of the plane, and we had the aisle and middle seat. I am an aisle-seat guy, suffering from a mild case of claustrophobia, and Vicki always gets stuck in the middle seat—sorry, I know this is not my most chivalrous moment.

The plane was almost fully boarded, and we'd scored—or so we thought, as no one had yet come to sit in the window seat. So, Vicki moved over, and we rejoiced in the small victory of a bit more room on a crowded flight, at a time when air travel is leaving us with ever-decreasing personal space.

Turns out, we did score but not in the manner we had thought or even hoped. You can probably visualize the scene. At the last minute, down the aisle came a really big guy with a full beard. At the risk of using a broad generalization, he looked like he definitely rode a Harley and was not to be messed with. He stopped next to me, looked at Vicki, and said, "I have the window seat."

We moved our stuff to the middle seat, and both got up and moved into the aisle so he could squeeze in, which he did, forcing his frame in a seat that was just way too small. As we moved to get back into our seats, I overheard him say to himself, obviously uncomfortable, "Oh, joy," and selfishly found myself thinking the same thing.

As happens to me often, especially when I get in my Drew-is-the-center-of-the-universe mode, I got slammed, big time. You can't judge a book by its cover, no kidding. Realizing that we were going to be fast friends at least for the next couple of hours, I tried to find common ground or a catchy phrase to break the ice. To my surprise, I saw in his cluster of reading material a best-selling novel that deals with one man's journey to meet God.

I asked, "What do you think of the book?" expecting a brief and simple answer.

Instead, I got something like this: "I love books that explore people's journey into a life of meaning. Not sure I like all the theology here, but it certainly got me thinking."

Uh, you serious, Clark?

Turns out the two-hour fight was not nearly long enough. We talked about a variety of topics relating to God and his life's work, which helps former prisoners acclimate into society. Just as we were landing, he told me that if I really wanted to read a good book, a tearjerker about how God works in all things, pick up *Same Kind of Different as Me*. By now, this guy had my attention, so we traded emails and contact information and I bought the book, which I ended up reading a few weeks later on our next airplane trip.

Oh boy, I still remember Vicki looking at me while I was reading it, as tears streamed down my face, asking me what was wrong. I just looked at her and mouthed, "I can't speak," which is rare for me. I ended up buying a bunch of copies of the book and gave them away to people in my life, something I like to do but only for books that I feel are unique and special. If you didn't get one, pick up a copy—but only if you are ready to cry and lose yourself in it for a while.

I also emailed my new friend to thank him for the recommendation, and we bantered for a while, then lost touch. But I think that is OK. Sometimes in life, we connect for a fleeting moment, sometimes for a season, and sometimes for a lifetime. The lesson here is pretty simple—saying yes even when we don't feel like it or see the upside often leads to some pretty cool things happening, things that are a heck of a lot more fun, a heck of a lot more meaningful than watching reruns or playing video games.

* * *

My wife's cousin Bradlee came to live with us when he was sixteen years old, along with his younger brother Cameron. Their parents are loving, good people but moved around a bit, and we just all agreed a little stability would be good for them, so our immediate family went from five to seven for a season.

The catalyst for this big decision and change was a conversation we had that July on a houseboat in Lake Shasta. Vicki and I are all about family. She grew up with an Italian father, so it was always about the family. My family growing up was not close, but I caught the bug. Each summer, we'd have some sort of family vacation, sometimes just the five of us but more often than not with grandparents and cousins—the more, the merrier.

The big lesson here for us parents is that you must have quantity time to get quality time. Being a good parent requires us to be selfless. I have witnessed firsthand the wreckage of families because parents spend more time doing their own thing than spending time with their kids, and sorry folks, but watching TV or posting on social media while they watch a movie on their iPad doesn't count.

We must not lose our way when leading our families. Stumbling in significant ways, or "backsliding," as it's called in Christian circles (which is vastly different from making mistakes, which we all do), can and typically will take our families down with us. God deals harshly with this type of behavior; Mark 9:42 says, "If anyone causes one of these little ones—those who believe in me—to stumble, it would be better for them if a large millstone were hung around their neck and they were thrown into the sea." A harsh word from God because being in a position of authority carries with it an extra weight of responsibility. No one forced us to have kids, so let's make it count.

I say all this not to be a tough guy but because I know that we as parents have the opportunity to help make our kids' dreams come true and that the magic happens at the most unexpected of moments. You cannot manufacture them; they just happen.

I still remember on one of our trips a few summers before "the houseboat" trip when we visited the San Juan Islands. It was here, nestled against a wooded forest on one side and a small cove and rocky beach on the other, when my father-in-law, Joe, and I created a treasure map and led the kids on a treasure hunt at dusk, an experience that is still talked about to this day. Of course, no treasure hunt is complete without a dare to take our kayaks out to the middle of the bay and jump off into the really cold and dark water.

Because the sun goes down late in the San Juan Islands in the summer, the barbeque for dinner did not get fired up until after 10 p.m., a little later than the usual 6 p.m. dinnertime for a family with three small kids. But hey, rules are made to be broken.

So, this summer was the houseboat trip, and sitting around the fire pit one night, on a small alcove where we were docked, telling stories, the idea that boys might come live with us during the school year was discussed. And by the end of August, they arrived suitcases and all.

Spencer was nine at the time, Jessie was seven, and Dani was four, so Vicki and I were in the sweet, innocent phase of parenting with playdates, sports, and other activities taking up most of our time. Our kids were all at the same school where we were volunteering and participating—life was full and simple.

To state the obvious, raising two teenage boys is quite different from raising three kids under the age of ten, even more so when they'd been raised by someone else (their parents) up until now. This was a huge season of growth for me as the decision to take in Brad and Cameron in, while beautiful in many ways, was full of sacrifice. Going from a pretty comfortable life that I was prepared for into unchartered territory was risky and stretched me a fair amount. My marriage grew stronger, and I think Vicki fell in love with me more as I grew as a man with a heart to help others. We prayed together more frequently than ever, asking God for direction and asking other parents we knew with older kids for wisdom. We were in over our heads and willing to get help wherever we could.

Brad was tough from the start. I think the origin of his frustration was that he was used to me being the fun cousin who took him on vacation and now I was the "parent" with the authority to make the rules—not so much fun anymore and quite the paradigm shift.

We were into bedtime stories, family dinners, and kid shows on TV with Dodgers and Laker games mixed in now that Spencer was nine and into sports. Not exactly an appealing lifestyle for a sixteen-year-old. Our goal was to maintain our family structure and values and continue to love on and pour into our children while at the same time supporting Brad and Cameron, making sure they truly felt like part of the family.

Upon their arrival, I set the ground rules—you've got to have boundaries. I am five foot nine, actually five foot eight and a half now that I am shrinking, so I will not pretend to be this big, physically imposing guy, but I can be intense and am not afraid of confrontation—maybe it's a short man's complex.

My general theme for the boys was that Vicki and I had never done this before. The rules we establish may be too strict. In fact, they probably would be to start. We could always change a rule, or the boys can lobby to change a rule for a period of time, but not in perpetuity. This was not a democracy; there were only two votes—Vicki's and mine. And never, ever, under any circumstances could a rule be disregarded or ignored. There were consequences if that ever happened, and I meant what I said.

Yes, Bradlee broke a few rules, I have learned that all teenagers break rules, even my sweet children. And yes, he suffered the consequences just like my sweet children.

Teenagers are full of drama. Everything is the end of the world, and I remember one afternoon when Brad asked if he could spend the night at his friend's house. We asked about supervision, and Brad said with a straight face that his friend lived with his older sister and her live-in boyfriend, both twenty-one, and they would be the ones providing supervision. "All is good," as he put it. We explained that the older sister and her boyfriend were not supervisors, but rather they were coconspirators, and he would not, under any circumstances, be spending the night there.

Oh my, you would have thought we beat him and locked him in a dungeon. Big crocodile tears and a tantrum that lasted about fifteen minutes, along with intermittent pleas to change the rules, just this time. He just couldn't get it together. When he finally went to his room, I remember Vicki and I looking at each other and asking, "Did we really sign up for this?"

I do not want you to get the impression that it was all rough sledding. We had some fun times and opportunities to celebrate achievements with the boys. With a nudge from Vicki and me, they both participated (albeit reluctantly at times) in our family's church life. But after a period of time, less than a year in Brad's case, we all recognized he needed to be with his parents. Work took his mom and dad to separate cities for a while, and Brad eventually moved back in with his dad. At the end of the day, I think it was just too tough for him to be away from them.

Vicki and I celebrated Brad's arrival, embraced his time with us, and exhaled a sigh of relief when he left. But that isn't the end of the story.

As a good-looking, highly likable young man, Brad eventually entered the social scene in Alabama, finding girls and bars to his liking. He shared his exploits now that I was back to being his cousin, and I would point him toward the life and example of Jesus.

In one conversation, he told me he would get to all this God stuff later; he was having too much fun. I told him the same thing I needed to hear when I was his age:

"You are assuming the greatest joy you can ever have is sex, booze, and rock 'n' roll, yet I know from experience that this simply isn't the case. Living a life of meaning alongside God and serving others is the greatest joy of all."

Knowing that Brad was listening and seeking, I spent a fair amount of time with him on the phone, walking him through the Bible as well as my journey—not just the good stuff, but the tough stuff as well.

Brad had been reading a copy of *The Purpose Driven Life* by Rick Warren, which I'd sent him earlier that fall, and on January 4, 2008, at a little before 9 p.m. Santa Barbara time or midnight Alabama time, I received a call from him. Seeing the time, I picked up the phone, a bit nervous about why he was calling. "All OK?" I asked.

He was emotional and said, "I got it, I finally got it, and from this day forward, I will live my life with God at the helm." And he has.

You serious, Clark?

I remember when we decided to take Brad and his brother Cameron in. More than a few people, even some people in our own family, said we were crazy, "You have a good life, why mess it up?" "Those boys were raised differently. It will be a nightmare." "Your marriage will fall apart." You get the idea.

Most of us have probably witnessed or been the recipient of critics or hecklers who give unsolicited, uninformed, and unhelpful advice at some point in our lives. When this happens to me and they really get on my nerves, I usually text or email them this excerpt from Teddy Roosevelt's famous speech "The Man in the Arena," hoping they both shut up and get moving.

> It is not the critic who counts; not the man who points out how the strong man stumbles, or where the doer of deeds could have done them better. The credit belongs to the man who is actually in the arena, whose face is marred by dust and sweat and blood; who strives valiantly; who errs, who comes short again and again, because there is no effort without error and shortcoming; but who does actually strive to do the deeds; who knows great enthusiasms, the great devotions; who spends himself in a worthy cause; who at the best knows in

the end the triumph of high achievement, and who at the worst, if he fails, at least fails while daring greatly, so that his place shall never be with those cold and timid souls who neither know victory nor defeat.

Yes, taking in Brad was hard. Most of the good stuff is. Yes, we messed up. All of us mess up.

Today, Brad is married to a wonderful lady and has three beautiful children. Today, Brad is a man who left behind the life that seduces many of us, the "sex, booze, party scene" and all that comes with it, for a life of family with God at the helm. He works hard and is a mentor to kids who are struggling, thus paying forward the blessings he received. Today, Brad is building a life full of love, service, and meaning.

A few years ago, he surprised his mom on her seventieth birthday by spearheading and organizing his entire extended family to show up and celebrate her. Today, Brad is a great man who is leading well. Sure seems like the hard work is worth it.

Chapter 22

Borena, Ethiopia, via Disneyland

The happiest place on Earth.
—Disneyland

A while back, while enjoying a few days of rest at a safari camp near the border between Kenya and Tanzania, our guide, Samson, told us that his work for the Maasai Wilderness Conservation Trust brought him to New York to run the New York City Marathon as part of a fundraiser and even to our hometown of Santa Barbara to tell his story. Small world for sure.

When we asked about his trip to the United States, he told us that the one experience he had that he just could not explain to his friends in the Maasai was Disneyland. No matter how hard he tried to paint the picture of all the rides and attractions, none of his friends could get their heads around what he was saying. Being from America, I never really thought about this before. Disneyland was just something you did, for me once a year, for others more frequently, but let's face it, everyone we know has been to Disneyland or least heard of it.

After returning home, we couldn't stop thinking about Samson's story and eventually made a pact that we would do our best to take people from Africa or other parts of the world to Disneyland whenever they came to stay with us.

I am not a Disneyland fanatic. Growing up, my kids knew they got to go once a year, typically in December before school was out and during the week to avoid the crowds. We would take them out of school, leave on a Tuesday, stay as long as they wanted, spend the night, and then stay as long as they wanted on Wednesday; that was it. Seemed like a fair deal—just enough time for them to get their fix and just enough time so Dad wouldn't lose his mind.

But despite my tempered love for Disneyland in moderation, I must admit it is pretty exciting to take someone there who has no expectations or reference point at all.

Our first foray into this trend was with our friend Moses from Kenya who came to visit us for a week one December. Early in our day after we had just entered the park and were walking down Main Street, not more than five minutes through the admission gates, I understood what Samson was saying. Navigating through the increasing number of people who were walking in and out of shops and indulging in various forms of junk food, Moses asked me, "Drew, where do all the people who live here go during the day when all these people are in their homes?"

OK, how do I explain this to a guy who lives in a village where a sign of wealth is having a cement floor in your house rather than a dirt floor? As I shared that no one actually lived at Disneyland, that this was a place people go for fun and that when it's closed, it's empty, he just couldn't get his head around it. He kept looking around at all the stuff and finally had to sit down on the curb and gather his thoughts. He couldn't fathom that a place like Disneyland, with all this cement, with all the solid roofs, walls, and fixtures, did not provide shelter to anyone.

It is important to note that Moses is a smart guy. He is an engineer who heads up Water Mission's Kenya program, employs lots of people, and runs a successful business. He just lives in a country in which excess is rare, and as the day went on, in the midst of the rides (which he loved) and food (which he loved a bit too much and paid the price for later), we talked about it all. Sitting for a moment next to a food stand with the giant turkey legs, we watched a family buy a couple of these legs, take a few bites, then toss them in the trash and stroll over to the churro stand. I am not being judgy, as we've all probably tossed out more food than someone in rural Kenya eats in a month, but I got the sense Moses would head back home and tell everyone about these crazy Americans.

* * *

A few years ago, our friend Saba asked us if her friend from Ethiopia, Pastor Tezera, could stay in our guesthouse for a week or so while he was visiting Santa Barbara. Her place was full, and Tezera wanted to fast and pray over the weekend and needed a quiet and private place to do so.

One of the great lessons Saba taught Vicki and me was to remember that at the end of the day, our house is really God's house, and it should be used to bless others. I still remember when she first started coming over. We were embarrassed and apologetic because our home was so much bigger than where she lived. But she encouraged us, telling us that there is nothing wrong with having a big house as long as it used to serve others—there is nothing wrong with having a big house, as long as we are willing to lose it.

We said yes, of course, and sure enough, when I came home from my office on Thursday, all the blinds in our little guesthouse were closed and Tezera was inside. Saba told us we could meet him on Monday when he was finished with his fasting and prayer time.

I am a prayerful person and understand the spiritual benefit of fasting. I pray daily and have fasted for a day on occasion over the years. But fast and pray from Thursday afternoon to Monday morning? Not so much. And if I am completely honest, if I go into my guesthouse to pray, I have maybe thirty minutes before I at least take a peek at ESPN, the news, or get distracted in some other way.

Monday morning, Saba was at our house bright and early, and Tezera walked out of the guesthouse and greeted us in a shiny suit and with a big smile. Like Saba, he is one of those people who just exudes love, and we had an immediate connection. Grabbing my hand with both of his hands, he thanked us emphatically for our hospitality. Warm handshakes quickly gave way to hugs, and we went inside for an espresso, eager to get to know our new friend. Tezera spoke English very well and had a certain savvy and understanding of the world that I honestly did not expect.

He shared his story, and we felt like we were getting a glimpse into life back in the early days of the church when people traveled by foot sharing all about Jesus. At the time, Tezera had started fifty-six churches that collectively have over twenty thousand members, all in the Borena region of southern Ethiopia.

To help provide a visual of how this looks and how it is vastly different from our churches in America, only nine of the fifty-six churches have buildings; the other forty-seven are simply outdoor gathering spots, typically under a tree to get some shade and relief from the intense desert heat. Tezera typically traveled by foot, walking through the bush, spreading the love of Jesus, and training up new pastors. More recently, he has been able to travel by jeep some of the time, although this mode of transportation is unreliable, and maintenance is difficult. He carries with him a few modest belongings, a Bible, and a small inflatable pool that he blows up and fills with any water he can find to baptize people.

Eventually Saba and Tezera headed off, and we made plans to reconvene that evening for dinner.

Vicki always stocks the refrigerator and cupboard in the guesthouse when we have people staying, and she did a quick check of the place, making sure Tezera had enough food for the rest of the week.

Forgetting that he'd fasted for about four days, she came back inside and shared with me that none of the food we left him was touched. We got the sense that these lengthy fasts were both without compromise and quite commonplace Pastor Tezera's life.

It was during this visit that we decided it was Saba and Pastor Tezera's turn to experience all that Magic Kingdom had to offer. With our kids older now and less willing to miss school, it was just the four adults, something I never would have done under normal circumstances. Saba, despite living in Santa Barbara, had never been to Disneyland, and she greeted the Disneyland parking lot by taking pictures and telling us how amazing it was. I stole Rodney Dangerfield's line from *Caddyshack* and said, "Saba, it's a parking lot."

Starting with an easy ride and one of my favorites, Soarin' over California, turned Tezera into a little kid wanting more, while Saba turned into a little kid wanting less. She was terrified of the "serious" rides and only wanted one thing while at Disneyland: a picture of her with Cinderella.

I still have the image of Saba, almost six feet tall, standing in line to get her picture taken alongside all the little girls. For a time, all she kept by her bedside was a Bible and that photo.

Tezera, on the other hand, could not get enough of everything. Vicki and I took turns taking him on a ride while the other one walked around with Saba, just soaking in the experience. Vicki and Tezera went on Space Mountain, which is Vicki's favorite, and Tezera just kept saying, "Wow, wow. This must be what Heaven is like."

I got to take him on California Screamin', the rollercoaster with a 360 loop that takes riders upside down. At the end of the ride, we checked out the cheesy photo they take and offer to sell to you for something like fifty bucks. When the kids were growing up, I would never buy any of these photos, thinking of them as a rip-off, and would even take a picture of the picture, which freaked them out. They, along with Vicki, accused me of being cheap, while I stuck to my guns, claiming solid stewardship.

But in this case, I made an exception and bought the photo of Tezera and me, hands in the air, grinning from ear to ear. He held on to it the rest of the day as if it were a prized possession. Little did I know then that the photo truly was valuable in a completely unexpected way.

Back in Ethiopia, several months after our trip to Disneyland with Tezera, he got in touch with us and told us that this photo was attracting a great deal of interest from the people he was meeting. In much of this area, tribes living deep in the bush have been in conflict with one another for thousands of years, not always on the scale of a full-on civil war, but always involved in one skirmish or another, usually over who's in charge of land, water, religion—the typical causes of strife. Many of the tribes also believe that there are multiple gods—with certain animals being revered as supreme deities.

Well, many of the local leaders just couldn't get enough of our picture. They couldn't believe that there was a contraption that goes that fast, that we could go upside down in this "thing" and not fall out and die, and that a white man and a black man could sit together on this ride holding hands in joy. As Tezera explained, there is still a stigma among tribes in parts of Africa regarding white people and black people interacting.

Long story short, people were literally dropping their weapons, pastor Tezera was starting more churches, and more lives were being changed. All because God's love shows up in crazy, out-of-this-world ways when we say yes, yes to Saba, yes to Tezera, yes to Disneyland, and yes to that cheesy photo. All these yeses added up to Borena, Ethiopia, becoming the happiest place on Earth.

Chapter 23

In the Blink of an Eye

Don't count the days, make the days count.
—Muhammad Ali

I no longer remember the exact month I went back there or the exact location, as it happened a long time ago. It was probably sometime during the late winter or spring of 1980, but when I stood looking down the steep canyon, my stomach dropped. How on earth did I survive this?

The evening started in a typical way for a Saturday; two of my high school buddies and I drove over the hill into Westwood to hang out and maybe see a movie. In Westwood, we met a group of girls who invited us back to one of their parent's houses in the hills not too far away.

Upon arrival at her house, we were greeted by her older brother and his friends, who were home from college and "encouraged" us to be on our way. I prefer to think we were intelligent, pragmatic young men who showed restraint in our pursuit of new friends, not wimps who cowered at the first sign of confrontation. Regardless, we were soon on our way.

Hopping into one of my friend's Mercury Bobcat, which, along with the Pinto, was the death trap car of this era, we headed down the canyon toward the freeway and home.

The older brother and his friends pulled out behind us in their big truck as an escort and probably to intimidate us a bit. No big deal, but for some reason, my friend panicked, thinking they were going to run us off the road, and started speeding up and taking the turns way too fast in an attempt to get away. We hadn't been drinking (if we had, I would say so), but regardless, the next thing I knew, we were tumbling down the mountainside.

Riding shotgun without a seatbelt was not the smartest thing I'd ever done, and while I do not remember the actual crash, I do remember "waking up" a ways down the hillside, and all of us stumbling out of the car, mostly in one piece. Shock does crazy things to people, and I remember my friend in the back seat who was the toughest of all of us (in fact, the only tough guy among us) telling me to make sure I threw the first punch if those guys were still around that when we got back up to the top of the canyon. *Yeah, sure; I got this.*

Not knowing how much time had passed, when we finally clamored back up to the road, there was quite a crowd, and of course no one was looking to fight us. They were all looking to help us. As I mentioned in my introduction, it turns out we'd hit a parked car before going over the cliff—a Cadillac with a couple inside admiring the view and likely doing what couples in cars do. Thankfully, they were OK, and their parked car being in that exact spot probably saved our lives.

One of the girls we followed home looked at me and said, "Oh, Drew, your face!" Obviously, I could not see it myself, but bringing my hand to my cheek, I found out it was covered in blood. That was enough for me, and I quickly said "OK" to some guy who offered to take us to the hospital. Hopping in shotgun again—what am I, stupid?—off we went. By the time we noticed the empty beer cans on the floor and realized this guy had a few, it was too late. I remember thinking to myself, *Well, we didn't die in the first crash, but maybe we will now.* Seriously, this is a true story: we crashed, *then* got into a car with a drunk guy to go to the hospital.

Thankfully, we made it, and as we were going through a series of tests to make sure we were OK, the police arrived.

I still remember to this day the first thing that the officer in charge said: "I wish you kids would stay off those canyon roads. Last weekend, we pulled three kids out of a car in a similar spot and all three were dead."

Talk about a wake-up call.

We were lucky. My friend in the back seat was unscathed. My other friend, the driver, had a small, Harrison Ford–like scar on his chin from hitting the steering wheel, which added, not detracted, from his looks. And I, despite all the blood from small, superficial cuts, was fine other than a concussion, which took me out of playing in soccer games for a while. Obviously, we ended up much better off than the guys who'd crashed a week earlier.

* * *

Almost forty years later, at around two thirty in the morning on January 9, 2018, a couple of weeks after our community endured the ferocious and devastating Thomas Fire, the slow, steady, almost calming rain changed almost instantly to a ferocious and ultimately destructive deluge. It pelted down with such velocity that, in some places, as much as one inch of rain fell in a fifteen-minute span.

The hills above tiny Montecito and the sought-after 93108 zip code, home to an array of celebrities and captains of industry, starved for vegetation after the recent fires, gave way, turning this idyllic enclave into a disaster area in just a few short hours.

Flash floods are uncommon to begin with and certainly not expected in our town. Generally, they happen in faraway places without the infrastructure to withstand them. Yet, on this night, tragedy struck in the form of water, mud, and boulders the size of cars rambling through the streets, destroying everything in their path.

Mother Nature is indiscriminate, and this mudslide was no exception. The people who died during this tragedy came from all walks of life: the super rich, the moderately well-off, and the poor. Homes on some streets were fine, while just a hundred feet away, there was nothing left: homes completely wiped out, torn right off their foundations and washed away.

Without living here, it is hard to imagine the destruction. It is even more difficult to grasp that our friends and neighbors could go to sleep, nestling in the warmth of their beds, safe from the rain, like always, only to be woken up by the surreal and thunderous rumbling of rocks, cars, trees, and water headed toward them with such speed that they and their homes were literally swept away in the blink of an eye.

* * *

Santa Barbara and the surrounding communities of Goleta, Montecito, Summerland, and Carpinteria (or Carp as it is called by us locals) is a small town, smaller in feel than in actual population. Families know one another from school, sports, church, the beach, and summer camps as well as the arts and a variety of other social outlets.

As such, this tragedy affected everyone. Obviously, those who lost family members were impacted the most, followed by those who had their homes destroyed or damaged. But even beyond that, shop owners and restaurants couldn't open, and the workers who serve the residents of our town—from hair stylists to gardeners to waiters and waitresses—could no longer do their job or make a living.

I remember when I first moved to Santa Barbara, someone told me that the reason there is so little crime here is because there are only three roads in or out—north or south on the highway and east over the pass into Santa Ynez. All law enforcement had to do was shut down those three roads, and the culprits would be trapped.

True, yes (and comforting, I guess), but now, with the freeway to the south closed, we were isolated. Friends in Carp wanting to comfort and help, as well as workers living just down the 101 in Ventura, could not get here. Grocery trucks bringing in food and water from

Los Angeles were forced to stand by or take the long way around, resulting in the usually one-and-a-half-hour drive now taking up to eight hours.

Even those of us not acutely impacted by the disaster, my family among them, were in a state of shock. About a week after the tragic events took place, we took a long bike ride and ended up discussing how we felt guilty that we were doing something nice for ourselves when just a few miles away, so many were hurting. We understood the old saying "life goes on'" and that we must keep on moving, but what we were doing just felt weird and inappropriate. I know many others felt the same.

As is the case in most calamities, our flood brought out the best and the worst in humanity, but mostly the best. The first responders who definitely needed some rest after fighting the fires were the true heroes, as they always are. Risking their own lives to rescue people who were stranded and search for survivors reminds us of their bravery and selflessness. I still hold on to the image of a firefighter with his fire hat and a wet suit wading through the mud in a parking garage that served as catch-all for much of the massive slide.

Some restaurant owners paid their staff even when they couldn't work, and people all over town opened up their homes to provide people with shelter for a night, or a week.

Our church, which meets in a converted old warehouse with a giant flat, rectangular parking lot, became the LAC (short for local assistance center), and the host to FEMA, insurance companies, the food bank, and numerous other nonprofits and organizations that were offering guidance and assistance to those impacted by the flood.

Each Sunday afternoon after church, a group of volunteers removed our pews, which are really just a bunch of wood benches, and replaced them with tables for each of the organizations that were part of the assistance efforts. Then they moved the tables out and benches back in on Saturday afternoon so we could have church on Sunday morning.

For sixteen days, every Monday through Saturday, people from all walks of life, some who had never or would never enter a church, showed up confused, broken, and seeking help. While the many organizations present there offered pragmatic assistance, our greeters offered love, a hug, a shoulder to cry on, a prayer.

Once again, the disaster was indiscriminate about who it impacted. The affluent never wanting for much in the way of comfort or security were now desperate and sitting alongside the small local business owners who were oftentimes sobbing and trying to figure out how they were going to pay their rent.

Through it all, and following God's word in 1 John 4:11 that reads, "Dear friends, since God loved us, we also ought to love one another," we as a church just loved on the people who came through our doors, offering a safe place for people to mourn, a place where they could get help, a place where they could ask for prayer, and a place where they could connect with others who were either sharing in their pain or offering a way back.

* * *

So, why do I share these stories about my car crash and the devastating flood in my hometown? They are not meant to try and answer the impossible questions of why the other guys died falling off the same cliff while my friends and I lived with few scars or long-term repercussions, or why some folks lost their lives in the mudslides while their next-door neighbors were left unscathed, nor is it to end things on a downer in what I hope has been a mostly inspirational read. Rather, these stories are to remind everyone that life is short and often shorter than we think. So how do we make it count?

At the core, what is life about?

- *Playing it safe and being comfortable or taking risks and living an adventure with others in mind?*
- *Getting more stuff or giving away more stuff?*
- *Success and recognition or significance and service?*

While certainly not knocking comfort, stuff, or recognition as bad in and of themselves, I think we lose when we make them the mainstay of our existence, the things that we worship or obsess over.

* * *

Reflecting in this way led me to another question that has been thrown around for years in slightly different variations:

If you knew you only had a short while to live, what would you do?

The idea is that if our answer is something different from what we are currently doing, we should change course and live that way now, not just when we know time is running out. While I think that this is an oversimplification of reality—we all have different seasons in our lives and shouldn't just drop out of school, quit our jobs, or set sail around the world at a moment's notice—I do believe that there is a valid point being made here, one worth considering: *What does a life that counts look like? What truly brings us the greatest joy?*

Thinking through how we choose to live the life we've been given requires us to yearn for life's meaning and search deep in our souls and ask ourselves the tough questions, a small sampling of which is below.

- *What gets me out of bed in the morning?*
- *What do I with the 86,400 seconds I am given each day? Do I spend time sweating the small stuff or dreaming about and acting on the big stuff?*
- *Am I asking what do I want from life, or what does life want and need from me?*
- *Am I sharing my piece of pie with others or keeping it to myself?*
- *When was the last time I ran with abandon to that sweet spot where the world's deep hunger and my deep gladness meet?*

Answering these questions and others like them truthfully matter, and I think they matter a great deal. *Does my life count in a lasting and meaningful way? Should I stay the course or change the course?*

My hope is that you take the time to ask yourself the big questions and live a life where you say yes, a life full of joy, purpose, and adventure, the life God has called you to lead, nothing less.

Afterword

Going the Distance

Endurance is not just the ability to bear a
hard thing, but to turn it into glory.
—William Barclay

The song "The Distance," written and performed by the band Cake, has a couple of lines about going the distance and going for speed. It kind of reminds me of a less well-known version of "Eye of the Tiger," which hit the scene as the theme song for Sylvester Stallone's third *Rocky* film, as both songs are high-energy pick-me-ups pushing us to win the contest or finish the race strong.

For years, my wife glommed on to the phrase "going the distance" as a way to challenge herself and her friends when she was in her running marathons season of life.

Lately, she has used it as her rallying cry to beat cancer.

* * *

By now, if you read Vicki's foreword and are still tracking with me through the pages of *Sweet Pecan Pie*, you know that she was diagnosed with colon cancer in August of 2023. I suppose the official report did not come out until after her surgery in early September, but we all knew before then. The tumor was too big, the doctors were too concerned, and the blood tests were too out of whack for things to be normal.

All this was never supposed to be part of this book; one can't prepare for cancer, or any disease or tragedy that comes out of nowhere, but once it happened, it seemed appropriate to add it to pages that hopefully highlight the important stuff in life and do a good job of inspiring all of us to live selflessly, regardless of circumstances.

It has given me an opportunity in real time to share the lessons learned from my wife, who is my biggest hero this side of Jesus. I think it completes the story, showing her heart during life's gnarliest of trials, and, in a weird way, I feel like the original publishing process was held up so this part of our life can be shared and hopefully inspire others. My guess is that her story (this part of my story) will have the greatest impact, and I tease her that no one will want to hear from me, but just about everyone will want to hear from her—which, by the way, would be awesome and just fine.

* * *

We were at the point where the 101 highway hits Ventura, right after the long stretch of road that is surrounded by the ocean on one side and rolling hills on the other, where motor homes are typically stacked adjacent to the beach regardless of the time of year. Cell coverage is spotty in this section of the Southern California coast, and missed or dropped calls are pretty much the norm.

Back in range, the phone rang. It was the doctor's office. Both our stomachs dropped, not really wanting to pick up but knowing we had to get *the* news sooner or later.

It was Thursday, August 24, a little before noon, less than twenty-four hours after her first blood test and scan. The CEA markers, which are one indicator of cancer levels in the body, had come in late yesterday afternoon. They were high, really high, leading to the longest and probably worst night of my life. I still remember Vicki, Mrs. Positive to the core, saying, "Honey, am I really sick?" and me thinking for the first time, *Maybe you are.*

The scary marker numbers came out of nowhere. We were really expecting this to be the "run-of-the-mill" early-stage colon cancer—serious for sure, but with surgery, we would be on our way and life would move on. Crazy how one data point can just blow up your plans and change your life.

Then again, I always remember the saying that was especially prevalent when our kids started to drive: "We are all just a phone call away from being on our knees."

So, here we were, driving south to pick up some things for our church remodel, when the phone rang. In typical Vicki fashion, she had to keep moving and do something for others to get her mind off what was going on.

I am not sure which I prefer: the "surprise" call (like the one from the afternoon before) that gives the news you never expected, or the "next" call for which you have anxious anticipation, knowing the news will either be bad or good, or maybe somewhere in between. I guess neither call is ideal.

"The scan looks good; it does not show cancer moving anywhere else in the body," were words that offset the news from Wednesday afternoon, and in the world of medicine and other areas of science, physical evidence carries more weight than the less reliable, somewhat nebulous data points such as blood tests. Knowing this and feeling like we had won the lotto, even for just a moment, Vicki started to sob, which was one of the few times I have seen her cry throughout this entire trial. I bawled like a baby, which seems to be my new norm. Go figure: the one who cries for no reason gets cancer and stops crying, and me, who rarely tears up, can't get it together.

This rollercoaster of news—bad news followed by good news, followed by so-so news—is part of the cancer journey, but to be fair, it is also part of life in general, which always has its ups and downs. These last number of months, more than any other time in my life, have been a reminder to stay strong, be courageous, and endure regardless of whether things are going well or not. Thankfully, my wife is a great example to follow and sets the bar high, as she runs with a smile regardless of what life throws at her.

* * *

The surgery took place the following Friday, two weeks after her original doctor's appointment, ten days after her colonoscopy, and a little over a week after her first of many tests. Things just happened so fast. In one way, we were embarrassed, as we felt like we cut in line ahead of other folks who were in the same boat, and in another way, we wished we had more time to process things.

Colon surgery takes five-plus hours and is not so fun when you sit around and have no idea of what's going on. Hearing from the surgeon that the tumor was "underwhelming" was a win, and the path report showing cancer was in two of the thirty-one lymph nodes removed was both win and a loss. A loss because chemo was in our future, but a win because had the number been higher, her treatment would've been twice as long and her long-term prognosis not nearly as good.

It's weird sitting on this side of things. Life goes on for others (as it should) while our life is upside down. A. A. Milne, the author of the timeless *Winnie-the-Pooh* series, once said, "If you live to be a hundred, I want to live to be hundred minus one day, so I never have to live a day without you," and that is certainly how I feel about Vicki.

I don't share this to try and prove I'm the most chivalrous guy ever. I'm not. I'm just making the point that women are tougher than men, that we should go (die) first, and that most of us men, at least those of us worth anything, would change places with our wives or kids if they were hurting in a nanosecond. Watching her suffer and feeling helpless is the worst, and at times I cry out, "Pick me instead. Pick me."

Then again, if it were me, I would never be as strong or selfless as Vicki, and the good stuff she is doing along the way wouldn't be here. So, most of the time, I have a peace that comes from the Bible in Romans 8:28, that God works all things for good.

* * *

In Drew's dictionary, away from Webster's, Dictionary.com, or the thousands of places we can go nowadays to get a word's meaning, endurance and courage are related. You can't run the race with energy, distance, and others in mind, especially in the midst of cancer or any hardship, if you're not courageous.

One of Mark Twain's quotes reads, "Courage is resistance to fear, mastery of fear—not absence of fear." I am pretty sure he understates Vicki's approach to this season of life, as she really has been fearless pretty much all of the time. And not with naïve optimism, but with a faith that she often verbalizes by reminding everyone who is scared and concerned for her that "God's got this."

I remember someone early in Vicki's diagnosis asking, "Why you?" to which Vicki responded, "Why not me?" Lots of friends, some close, some more of acquaintances, seem surprised and even shocked that Vicki is living such a full and generous life while not feeling at the top of her game and facing a future full of uncertainty. Others asked, in one way or another, "How on earth do you take those three pills every morning and every night, which basically make you feel awful, and walk right into a full day of doing stuff, good stuff, meaningful stuff? How do you keep moving so fast?"

Her courage comes through her faith and her grateful heart. I think, at the core, courage in general stems from hope and gratitude—being thankful for each day and avoiding the "feeling sorry for one-self" mindset that tends to creep into the lives of those of us who have it easy when we encounter even the smallest inconvenience.

When we're grateful, we can extend ourselves to others rather than seek more for ourselves. Some may say that this is much easier to do in times of prosperity than the other way around. But I have found that most of the time, circumstances are not correlated to gratitude or lack thereof. You either run with a grateful heart or you don't, and trust me, (or better yet, trust Vicki): joy is an extension of gratitude, 100 percent.

* * *

Every third Monday, she makes her way to the cancer center to have her blood drawn. Emails with test results follow as all of her "levels" are checked to make sure she is tolerating the treatments without too much strain on her body.

The next day, we are back at same place together to meet the doc or PA, provide them with an update on how she feels, and then head into the room where treatments are given. The facility itself is nice, the chairs are comfortable, and the setting tries its best to be peaceful, but you just feel the despair walking in. There is a dramatic contrast between the providers and the patients, as the nurses are full of smiles and so helpful, while the patients do their best to avoid eye contact and drift into their own little world.

Most of the folks receiving treatment are alone, and almost all have a coat or blanket around them, as one of the main side effects of the drugs being administered is that weird cold sensation that makes it difficult to hold anything that is not warm to the touch. The chairs in the room that are the more isolated and private are usually full when we arrive, as most people there want to keep to themselves.

Vicki takes a different approach, hopping into the chair right in the middle of things. I stay a few minutes, then one of her friends joins her and they visit, pray, and read together, bringing a ray of sunshine into the darkness for the three hours or so she is in there. Even when feeling a little out of it as she leaves, she waves goodbye with a smile, a thank you, and a small gift of appreciation. I imagine most of the other patients think she is crazy, but Vicki is living the same way she did before cancer came along, albeit with a few more appointments and an earlier bedtime.

The IV itself has side effects—namely, a sore arm, which, like the hands, face, and teeth, hurts for a week or so after treatment day. Then it is two weeks of pills (three in the morning and three at night), a week off, then rinse and repeat. Food is unappealing, as is water (I have no idea why, but she says it tastes like metal), so meals are not exciting; they're more of a means to take her medicine on a full stomach, and warm tea is her liquid of choice.

When she has her moments when a little rest will help, she responds to every text of prayers and well wishes with a personal note—not just a generic "cut and paste" response but something that is unique and special to each person. And when she is on the move, you'll find her serving in our church and community, and even crawling on her hands and knees (figuratively, of course) to New York City to watch both our daughters run the New York City Marathon twenty years after she accomplished the same feat.

* * *

If courage is derived from hope and gratitude, it most certainly leads to empathy, and I think both of us have new eyes for those folks who have it rough. I know Vicki looks around and sees a world full of hurting people, people who have it worse than her.

Early in her diagnosis, we were made aware of a single mom with three kids, a 9–5 job, and stage 4 cancer. The thought of her all alone and being so sick with a full schedule and a challenging outlook made us super sad and got us thinking about the extra challenges those lacking in resources and margin have when facing something difficult that disrupts their routine. We wondered about the backup plan for her children if things turned south and thought, *How we can complain or feel sorry for ourselves when this poor lady has it so much worse?*

Later, when we got the reminder for Vicki's Tuesday before Thanksgiving time slot for an IV drip, it listed the start time as 1 p.m. Thinking earlier is better, especially right before Thanksgiving, she called and asked if there were earlier times available, only to be told that with the holiday, treatments are stacked into fewer days and the people given the early times are those with six- to eight-hour treatments. Imagining an IV two to three times as long as Vicki's made us both sick to our stomachs and once again reminded us to be grateful for where we are.

Throughout all this, our dear friend Beste has spent the last year getting rides back and forth to the hospital to sit and hold the hand of her husband, who was in a terrible car accident and still requires around-the-clock care, while also raising their young son. She tackles all this without family close by, in a country that is new to her, where she struggles with the language and the culture. Yet, our regular FaceTime calls are met with a time of sharing, prayer, and hope. Beste, like Vicki, finds her strength through her trust in God and is resilient and courageous while enduring impossible circumstances.

There are countless stories like the ones above; these are just a couple that have touched us. If you don't know it now, here's the wake-up call. Life is messy, and everyone has a few bumps in the road. Some are worse than others, and some are really hard to understand or conquer, but it's how we choose to deal with them that ultimately determines our attitude, our ability to persevere, and our impact on the world.

* * *

Cancer gets its fair share of press, and rightfully so, as it is a destructive and insidious disease. We read about the famous folks who overcome or succumb to some form of cancer, and there are all kinds of fundraisers and capital campaigns to fund research and find a cure.

It has been an interesting study to observe how people respond to hearing that you have cancer; sympathy and concern, of course, are quite common and super sweet. We have been surprised to hear

"Welcome to the cancer club" uttered more than a few times, realizing so many folks have been impacted by cancer at some point. And while Vicki, or anyone for that matter, would rather join a different club, there is a peace to belonging that comes from community. I think this is true all the time but even more so when things are tough.

Belonging is a huge part of the human condition, and empathy leads us into the arms of others both when we need help and when we are ones helping out. Finding your "peeps" is huge, especially so when the going gets tough, whether it be with your biological family, peers, or a small group of like-minded people who have your back.

* * *

Late in Dave Brown's life, as he battled cancer, he and his wife, Jane, invited Vicki and me over to their place for a visit. Dave was a leader in the early days of our local church, sort of a grand pooh-bah who has influenced and mentored so many leaders over the years.

He was a landscaper by vocation but was defined by the work he did to help others and his love for his Lord and his wife. As the four of us sat adjacent to his garden having some tea and cookies "al fresco" in typical Santa Barbara style, and knowing his days on earth were numbered, he asked about the state of the church: What did we think? Was it healthy? Churches, like all organizations, have different seasons, both good and not so good, and he wanted to make sure our church, where he had served for decades, was in a good place and in good hands as he went on to Heaven.

Vicki and I learned that he was having these short visits with a handful of folks, one by one, on the days he felt good enough to get up, chat, and share. Then, in typical Dave fashion, he told Jane: "That is enough visits—the rest of my days are for you."

We were honored to get that time with him, and I reflect often on the beauty of his intensity and focus on others even as he was dying. As we left that day and in the days that followed, I also thought about my wife's favorite saying to me when I am chasing a goal or objective, entirely focused on getting it over the finish line: "Honey, stop and smell the roses." In short, she is always reminding me to enjoy the ride and time with others, not just the outcome. Seems like sound advice and something I am more aware of and committed to since cancer became part of our journey.

* * *

Gratitude, hope, courage, empathy, and community. Find the right mixture of these five things and you will have the recipe to endure whatever comes your way and live a purposeful, adventurous, and joyful life.

As Vicki encourages me often, it is a lot more fun to "go the distance" with a happy heart, giving life everything we've got.

A footnote on Vicki:

This chapter was written during the tail end of her treatments, and as I type this footnote on Christmas Day, she is getting ready to toss the small container that held those awful but necessary cancer pills into the trash for the last time.

As you read this, we will be firmly planted in the post-cancer-treatment land of tests and scans, making sure that the cancer is gone, never to return. After some tough early days during this part of our journey, Vicki's long-term prognosis is good, for which we are grateful.

A footnote on cancer and the other tough stuff:

I spend a fair amount of time in this chapter and throughout the book highlighting some of the people whom I admire for their courage and purpose during difficult circumstances.

By no means am I unsympathetic for the times in life that people just can't keep moving because they are too sick, too broken, or too old. In those cases, may the rest of us care enough to help and run for them.

Acknowledgments

There is a great scene in the movie *Tin Men* starring Danny DeVito and Richard Dreyfuss as Ernest Tilley and Bill "BB" Babowsky, who are rival aluminum sliding salesmen in Baltimore back in the early 1960s. The banter in this movie is over-the-top funny, and in this scene, dubbed the "*Life* Magazine Scam," Richard Dreyfuss and his partner are set up with a tripod and a camera in the front yard of a typical suburban home. Curious, the lady who lives there walks out and asks them what they are doing. To which they reply, and I paraphrase here but you'll get the idea, that they are from *Life* magazine and are there to take a picture of her home, after which they will take a picture of another home that looks like her home only with aluminum siding and much more beautiful. She takes the bait and says she can't believe she is going to be in *Life* magazine, but can't her house be the after picture with aluminum siding instead of the before picture? And the anatomy of the perfect, not exactly honest but effective sales pitch is off and running.

I love this movie and this scene in particular, but when I think about it—big picture—this is what God does with me. He dusts me off, warts and all, and loves me unconditionally even when I mess up, which is quite often. I get to be the after picture in His eyes. The good news is I think we all get to be the after picture in His eyes if we give Him a chance. Don't know about you, but this sure sounds like a pretty good deal to me.

* * *

The Rascal Flatts version of "Life Is a Highway" is the perfect road trip song. It makes me want to take a long drive and sing out loud with the windows open and the top down. Let's go! It is also a good way to think about life in general. We ride this highway of life, and when doing it with people whom we love, respect, and share mutual interests with, we want to do it all night long.

With this in mind, a big thank you to everyone mentioned in the book, as well as many others who are not on the pages but are in my life or were at one time or another. All of you are people that I've been blessed to ride alongside, and my life is better, fuller from it.

I know that I could take up many pages just listing all of you who have encouraged me over the years and write a whole other book providing the details of how you impacted my journey. Some of these stories were already shared, while countless others live forever in my heart.

* * *

In no particular order, except saving my family for last:

Thank you, Pastor Harold and Carl, for spending over a year with me as I explored my beliefs, the universe, and pretty much asked every question possible as it relates to God. Your patience, commitment, and wisdom were gracious and instrumental in me ultimately deciding to throw my hat in the ring with Jesus.

After Pastor Harold, I have had three senior pastors in my life. Pastor Ricky—thank you for welcoming me into Calvary Chapel, believing in me, and encouraging me. I can still remember when I was struggling with being a late bloomer, and you got right in my face and said in a way only you can, "Doesn't matter. Look at you now." Pastor David—I am grateful for having an opportunity to learn from you and watch you lead with a humility that is rare, especially for people with such a wide reach and influence. Our trip to Israel under your leadership is one of the highlights of my life. Pastor Tommy—I have never met a more selfless man. Thank you for allowing me to run with you. The highway is much more fun with you on it.

* * *

Bob Shank, thanks for coaching me into a life of significance, I can't imagine a life without the principles I learned from you.

Pat Murdock, thanks for being gracious, wise, and a friend in the truest sense of the word. I value our time together and can only imagine what a world full of people like you would look like.

Skiffer, all I can say is you are a modern-day Apostle Paul, serving, loving, and leading in the midst of intense persecution. Thanks for teaching me and so many others about real faith and grace.

Biegs, I know you sit in Heaven with your big smile, contagious laughter, humor, and wit. I will always cherish the days we bantered and experienced life together. More to come on the other side.

* * *

Since this is a book that reflects on my journey and all my life experiences thus far, I have often found myself looking back to a time when my kids were little, a time that I fondly refer to as the ELMO years, named after the sweet, special school where they learned about God, where they were shaped with character and gained wisdom. ELMO was and still is an extension of our family, a place where we dreamed, played, served, and laughed together. It is a place that changed me forever in a good way. Thank you, Jeannine Morgan, for being our fearless and Godly leader for so many years, and thank you to each and every teacher and staff member for your dedication and love. Thank you to all those who served alongside Vicki and me in a variety of ways at different times, including the leaders who helped ELMO and Providence join together, ensuring Christian education thrives in Santa Barbara for years to come. The work you labored over is of great and lasting importance.

* * *

When I think about my work career, I still cannot believe how blessed I am to do what I do from sleepy Santa Barbara. Thank you to the leaders in the early days that allowed this to happen when working away from a big city was not the norm. And thanks to Brett, Ricci, Renee, Rich, Mitch, and all those I have worked alongside throughout the years. Running our business with excellence while still having time for family and purpose outside of work is something I will always be grateful for.

* * *

Thank you, John David and Kirsten, for always welcoming us to our home away from home. We love you guys and find our time together such a blessing: full of purpose, banter, and adventure.

* * *

Thanks to the guys who serve alongside me at Calvary Chapel Santa Barbara, including Bret Shellabarger, John Davies, Jay Stryker, Ed Ware, Ralph Murillo, Terry McElwee, and Ray Navarro, all of whom don't look at the golden years as a time to slow down, but rather as an opportunity to double down. We have been in service together for a number of years now, and I am grateful for our time together and the fellowship, trust, and unity that we have developed as brothers and co-laborers for God—thank you for leading by example.

A special shout-out to Dave Brown, who recently left us to spend eternity in Heaven. Your role as a leader in our church for so many years taught me many things, most importantly to love my wife the way Jesus loves us all. You set the bar high, my friend, and I aspire to be a better husband each and every day as a result of your example. And Jane—you model grace and faith in a way that draws people closer to God. It is really special to get a glimpse into the way you influence so many.

Gail and Jerry Gray, thank you for leading, serving, and teaching even during life's toughest of trials. Gail, thanks for smiling, making us laugh, and caring about Vicki and me as you battle ALS, and Jerry, thanks for showing me what it really means to live out the vow to love in both sickness and in health. You two are wonderful people, and I so value our friendship.

And all the pastors and staff, you bring excellence to everything you do; I am super stoked I get to yoke alongside you in this season.

* * *

For all of the volunteers who have served at H4O over the years, thank you for believing in our vision and mission. Lives in our community and all over the world were changed because of your dedication. To the Greene family, Kevin, Madison, Hector, Moses, and so many others at Water Mission—you are the best and, as far as I am concerned, the standard for how to match the heart of Jesus with the will and skill to make things happen. Thanks for being such thoughtful and generous hosts, allowing us to come in and be part of your efforts to end the world's water crisis.

And to the parents who trusted your kids with us as we journeyed to faraway places, thanks for taking a risk and letting us get to know them in a way we never could back home. A special thanks to all the young people who have stepped up, worked hard, and kept me young, or at least younger. It has been a privilege to hang out with you and do so with a shared desire to help others.

* * *

To my new band of brothers, Ian, Rob, Chad, Mark, and Daniel—crazy how we connected a couple of years ago for a few days in the mountains of Wyoming and Idaho and now are joined together in deep, meaningful ways as we encourage one another to live a life of generosity in the midst of crazy adventures. Love you guys and look forward to the many good times ahead.

* * *

Brent and Julianna—thanks for always having my back and for showing me what a generous life looks like. You are truly special people and special friends.

Keith, Beste, and Aslan—crazy how you walked into our home one summer and became part of the fabric of our family. We love you and are so grateful that we get to do life together (through the good stuff and the trials), even when we are six thousand miles apart.

Earl and Rhonda—thanks for being our safe and comfortable place, a place where we can "let our hair down," be ourselves, and love one another unconditionally, "warts and all," as you often say. We are grateful for our friendship that will last a lifetime.

Tommy and Debi—Vicki and I love to laugh, dream, serve, and pray together. We cherish the way we root for each other, celebrating the victories and holding on to one another during the trials. You make our lives better—always—and we love, love, love doing life together.

* * *

To John Pierce, who gave my mom a new lease on life, thank you for loving her and our family. Thank you for sharing your many life adventures with us. It was a special time with you around. Rest in peace, my friend.

To Joe and Alicia—the best in-laws I could ever ask for. You have a full and special relationship with your kids and grandkids because you are present, constantly lifting us up and loving on us. You make the effort, and all our lives are so much better for it. Love you both.

To my son, Spencer—thanks for being there for me at a time in your life when you are just getting going. I treasure our conversations as we banter about everything under the sun and sharpen each other. Your mom and I take great comfort in watching you honor God and honor your marriage. Shallon, thanks for loving our son and making him a better person. There is nothing the two of you can't do. And to the newest additions of our family, our first grandson, Blair Thomas Dusebout, and our first granddaughter, Eden Alice—welcome into the world and into our family. I can't wait for all the adventures in front of us and will cherish every moment we spend together.

To my oldest daughter, Jessie, you are a joy, a rare combination of heart and ambition. It is always a blast to be part of the many excursions you plan and a blessing to watch your compassion and service. Vicki and I could not be any prouder of you.

To Dani, the baby of the group, you have grown into a beautiful, confident, caring young woman, who has the innate gift of lifting others up and encouraging community. We love seeing how you build bridges and foster an environment where people can work together. We are beyond excited for this season of your journey.

And to Vicki, my soulmate and best friend who patiently listened to me fumble my way through a proposal thirty-four years ago and said "yes," the best yes of my life. Thank you for loving me, supporting me, rescuing me, and bringing me into a life of adventure and purpose. You are simply the best and toughest person I know.

Printed in the USA
CPSIA information can be obtained
at www.ICGtesting.com
CBHW020838120724
11350CB00011B/280